Everyday Home Repairs

Cy DeCosse Incorporated
Minnetonka, Minnesota

Contents

Introduction 5

The Basic Tool Kit 6
Tips for Choosing Tools 8
Tips for Using Screws & Nails 10

Repairing Windows & Doors 54

Installing New
  Weatherstripping 56
Repairing Loose or
  Sticking Windows 60
Replacing Glass 62
Replacing Screens 63
Repairing a Lockset ... 66
Door Latch Repairs ... 68
Freeing a Sticking
  Door 70

Repairing Walls & Ceilings 74

Fastening Objects to
  Walls or Ceilings 76
Repairing Wallboard ... 80
Repairing Plaster 82
Repairing
  Wallcoverings 84
Ceramic Tile
  Care & Repair 86

Copyright © 1988
Cy DeCosse Incorporated
5900 Green Oak Drive
Minnetonka, Minnesota 55343
1-800-328-3895
All rights reserved
Printed in U.S.A.

Also available from the publisher:
*Decorating With Paint & Wallcovering,
Carpentry: Tools • Shelves • Walls • Doors,
Kitchen Remodeling, Building Decks,
Home Plumbing Projects & Repairs, Basic
Wiring & Electrical Repairs, Workshop*
*Tips & Techniques, Advanced Home
Wiring, Carpentry: Remodeling,
Landscape Design & Construction*

Library of Congress
Cataloging-in-Publication Data

Everyday Home Repairs

(Black & Decker Home Improvement Library)
1. Dwellings - Maintenance and repair -
Amateurs' manuals. I. Title. II. Series.
TH4817.3.E93   1988   643'.7   87-30486
ISBN 0-86573-700-2
ISBN 0-86573-701-0 (pbk.)

CY DE COSSE INCORPORATED
Chairman: Cy DeCosse
President: James B. Maus
Executive Vice President: William B. Jones

EVERYDAY HOME REPAIRS
Created by: The Editors of Cy DeCosse
  Incorporated, in cooperation with Black
  & Decker. **BLACK&DECKER** is a trade-
  mark of Black & Decker (US), Incorporated
  and is used under license.

Basic Plumbing Know-how 14

Fixing a Leaky
  Faucet 16
Fixing a Running
  Toilet 24
Opening a Clogged
  Drain 28
Opening a Clogged
  Toilet 33

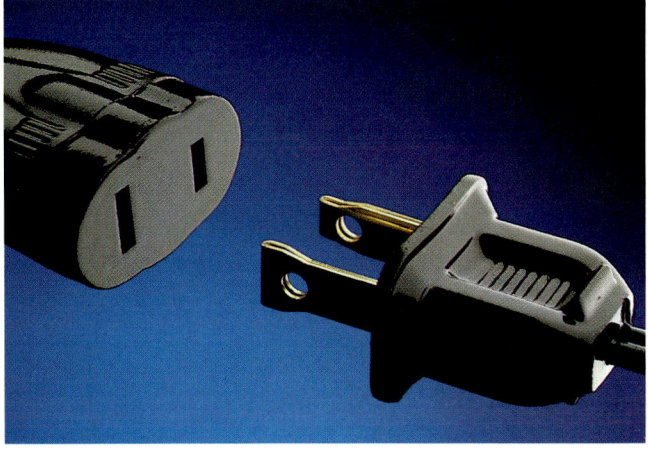

Basic Electrical Know-how 36

Electrical Safety 38
Replacing a Cord
  Plug 42
Replacing a Lamp
  Socket 44
Replacing a
  Receptacle 46
Replacing a Switch 48
Replacing a Light
  Fixture 50

Floor Repairs 91

Repairing Carpeting ... 92
Repairing Vinyl
  Floorcovering 94
Replacing Vinyl
  Floor Tiles 95
Repairing Hardwood
  Floors 96
Silencing Squeaky
  Floors & Stairs 98

Exterior Home Repairs 102

Fixing a Leaky Roof ... 104
Downspout & Gutter
  Problems & Repairs .. 110
Filling Cracks
  & Holes 116
Concrete Repairs 120
Asphalt Care &
  Repair 124

Index 126

Project Director: Gary D. Branson
Associate Creative Director: William Nelson
Editor: Bryan Trandem
Art Director: Barbara Falk
Project Manager: Barbara Lund
Project Consultant: Bernice Maehren
Production Manager: Jim Bindas
Assistant Production Manager: Julie Churchill
Production Staff: Janice Cauley, Joe Fahey, Carol Kevan, Yelena Konrardy, Dave Schelitzche, Linda Schloegel, Jennie Smith, Greg Wallace, Scott Winton, Nik Wogstad
Studio Manager: Cathleen Shannon

Photographers: Rex Irmen, Tony Kubat, John Lauenstein, Bill Lindner, Mark Maceman, Mette Nielsen
Contributing Photographers: Rudy Calin, Paul Englund, Dan Halsey, Michael Meyers, Charles Nields
Contributing Individuals and Manufacturers: Atlanta Sundries; Bondex International, Inc.; Cooper Industries (including registered trademarks: Crescent, Lufkin, Nicholson, Plumb, Turner, Weller, Wire-Wrap, Wiss, Xcelite); Dap, Inc.; Elkay Manufacturing Co.; Flameau Products Corp.; Goldblatt Tool Co.; H. B. Fuller Co.; Merle Henkenius;

Phil Hinz; 3M Home Products Division; Moen Faucets; Padco, Inc.; Peerless Faucet; Plano Molding Co.; Proko Industries, Inc.; Radiator Specialty Co.; Red Devil, Inc.; Sashco Sealants; Schmitt Music Centers; The Stanley Works; Wayne Swanson; TK Products, Division of Sierra Corp.; United Gilsonite Laboratories; USG Corp.; WD-40 Co.; William H. Harvey Co.; William Zinsser & Co., Inc.; Yale Security, Inc.
Printed on American paper by:
Ringier America, Inc. (0393)

Spout O-ring

4 Replace the entire cartridge if the faucet leaks. Do not attempt to replace only the O-rings or neoprene seals. Reinsert retaining clip; replace retaining nut.

5 Remove spout by pulling up while twisting. Cut off old O-rings using a knife. Spread heatproof grease on new O-rings before installing. Replace spout.

6 Lift lever

Introduction

Hourly labor costs for home repairs have risen beyond the budgets of many homeowners. Even if you are able to pay the current labor prices, finding someone to do the job right and do it when you need it done may be difficult. Today, improvements in tools and materials are helping put home repairs within the skill levels of all, and *Everyday Home Repairs* shows you the techniques that professionals use to solve the most common problems.

To find the information you need, turn to our Contents. Repair projects are organized under six basic categories, then broken down into more than 100 of the most common problems. Next turn to the page indicated for your problem. There you will find a "Before You Start" tip box that contains a list of all the tools and materials you will need to help you get started and to successfully complete each repair. The tip box serves as a checklist to help organize the project and avoid those last-minute trips to the store for forgotten repair items.

When you have assembled everything you need you're ready to start the repair. We've tried to present the repair steps as completely and as clearly as possible. There are no line drawings in *Everyday Home Repairs*. We actually performed each repair and took step-by-step photos to record the process completely and clearly. The result is that this book contains over 480 color photographs, more than 400 of which are instructional, how-to action photos.

What you see in the photos is what you will see when you take your faucet apart, or when you remove the cover from an electrical outlet. In addition to solutions to specific problems, you will find dozens of money-saving hints and helpful tool techniques, all guaranteed to make this the most helpful home repair book you can own.

NOTICE TO READERS

This book provides useful general instructions, but we cannot anticipate all of your working conditions or the characteristics of your materials and tools. For safety, you should use caution, care and good judgment when following the procedures described in this book. Consider your own skill level and the instructions and safety precautions associated with the various tools and materials shown. Neither the publisher nor Black & Decker® can assume responsibility for any damage to property or injury to persons as a result of misuse of the information provided.

The instructions in this book conform to "The Uniform Plumbing Code," "The National Electrical Code Reference Book" and "The Uniform Building Code" current at the time of its original publication. Consult your local Building Department for information on building permits, codes and other laws as they apply to your project.

Basic Power Tools

A few good-quality power tools can greatly expand your skills and level of satisfaction for home repair projects. Any project is faster and easier if you use a power tool. A ⅜" variable-speed reversible drill is one of the most versatile tools you can own: it can drill holes, screw in fasteners, file metal, strip rust and paint — even stir paint. A power jig saw with a variety of blades tackles just about any cutting job. A quality jig saw handles wood stock up to 2" thick. A circular saw with a blade diameter of 7" or more is an essential tool for carpentry projects. A pad sander simplifies wood refinishing jobs.

Circular saw

Saw blades

Pad sander

Power jig saw

Saw blades

Sandpaper

⅜" variable-speed drill

Drill bits

Tips for Choosing Tools

Buy both slot and phillips screwdrivers in a variety of tip sizes. Using the wrong screwdriver can damage the screw or the workpiece.

Do not use screwdrivers as chisels or prybars. A bent screwdriver shaft or a damaged tip can cause the screwdriver to slip and damage the workpiece.

Keep chisels and other cutting tools sharp. Forcing dull tools can be dangerous.

Natural bristle brushes provide a smoother finish for alkyd enamel or varnish coats.

Synthetic bristle brushes, such as this blend of nylon and polyester fibers, should be used for latex paints.

Inexpensive sponge brushes can be used on small paint or touch-up jobs, and thrown away when job is done.

Small line level, designed for leveling masonry walls, is also handy for leveling pictures or mirrors on walls.

Buy clamps to hold a workpiece securely while drilling or sanding, or for holding two pieces together until glue sets.

Fit shop files with handles to provide a safe and comfortable grip when working on metal. A variety of file shapes will let you work on any object.

Make a dent with a center punch to start a hole in metal. This will encourage the bit to stay on target.

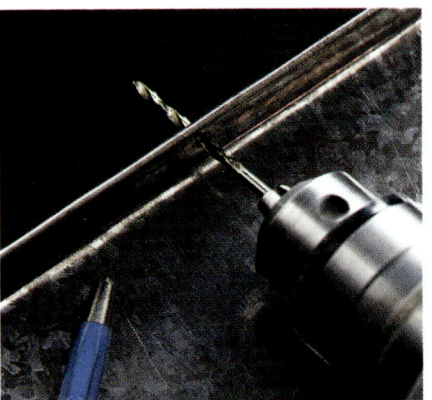
Use variable speed drill when drilling metal and keep rpms low to drill smoothly and to prevent dulling the bit.

Buy a variety of saws and blades to handle any repair task. The circular saw is a must for cutting heavy framing lumber; a jig saw can cut odd shapes.

Use a hot glue gun to secure corner braces or reinforcements, or to fasten small objects that might split if nailed.

Do not use a claw hammer as an all-purpose tool. It is designed only for driving and pulling nails.

Clean the hammer face with sandpaper to remove residue caused by coated nails. This reduces the number of bent nails.

The wide stiff blade of this quality measuring tape lets you measure without having a partner to hold the other end.

Professional jig saws have quality construction to stand up to hard use, and the versatility to accomplish any cutting job.

A combination square will mark 90° or 45° miter cuts on small workpieces. Use a carpenter's square (top) for larger framing lumber.

Tips for Using Screws

Screw assortment includes (left to right): flat and oval head wood screws, machine screw with nut, screw with washer for securing fiberglass panels, machine screw, sheetmetal screw, wallboard screw and lag screw.

Select a drill bit slightly smaller than screw shank diameter for drilling a pilot hole.

Pre-bore a pilot hole and countersink the screw head using this combination drill bit.

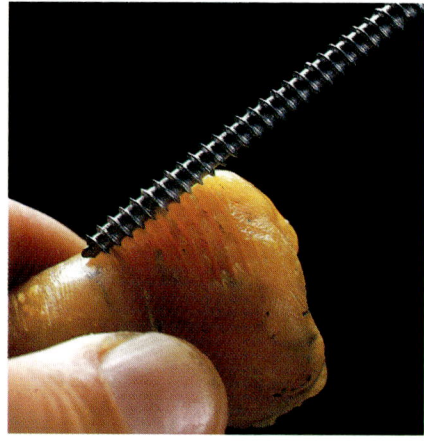

Lubricate a screw with beeswax for easier driving with a screwdriver or screwgun.

Choose the screwdriver that fits the slot in the screw head. The narrow blade of the driver at right may slip and damage the screw head.

Use a wooden golf tee or dowel to plug oversize screw holes in wood. Cut the plug off flush and drive in a new screw.

Flat or decorative wood buttons are available to cover and conceal countersunk screw heads.

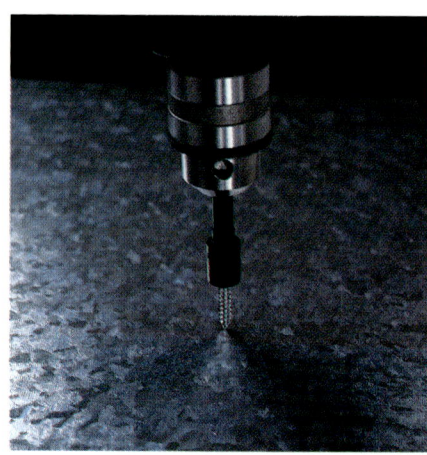

Drive self-tapping sheetmetal screws with an electric screwdriver or electric drill, with a hex socket.

Tips for Using Nails

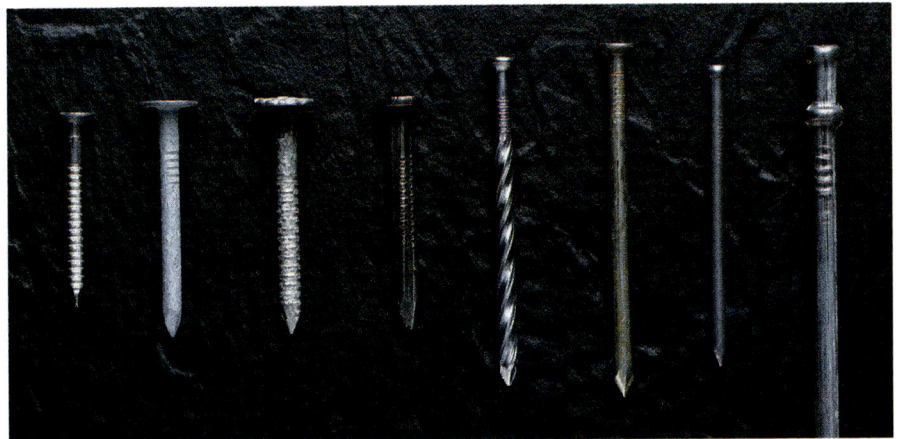

Nail assortment includes (left to right): wallboard nail, galvanized roofing nail, sealing roofing nail, concrete nail, hardwood flooring nail, common framing nail, finishing nail and double-headed form nail.

Predrill hardwood to avoid splitting it. Use a finishing nail as a drill bit for quick and accurate hole sizing.

Stagger nails so they do not all enter the same spot in the wood grain and split the wood.

Angling nails as shown will provide better holding power than driving them straight in.

Use the right hammer for superior job results. The tack hammer at rear is magnetized to hold tacks, and is lightweight to avoid damaging wood.

Toenailing is one method of joining two pieces of wood when end nailing is not possible.

Avoid damage to wood by using a nail set to drive the finish nail below the surface.

Use a brad pusher to position small nails in picture frames or other workpieces that might be damaged by a hammer.

Plumbing

Basic Plumbing Know-how

Materials for Plumbing

Tools for Plumbing ▶

The plumbing lines running through your home include two separate systems of pipes. The **freshwater supply** pipes are narrow, ½ to 1 inch in diameter, feeding clean water to all parts of your house under pressure. The **drain-waste-vent** (DWV) lines run through large pipes, 1¼ inches or more in diameter, into the sewer. The drain system is under no pressure; it operates by the force of gravity.

Nearly all plumbing repairs involve **leaks** or **clogs**. Leaks are caused by the pressure in the supply system which puts stress on the pipes, joints and fixtures. Clogs form because of the lack of pressure in the drain system.

The following pages introduce the basic plumbing techniques. The first rule of successful plumbing repair: shut off the water and drain the pipes before beginning.

How to Shut Off the Water & Drain the Pipes

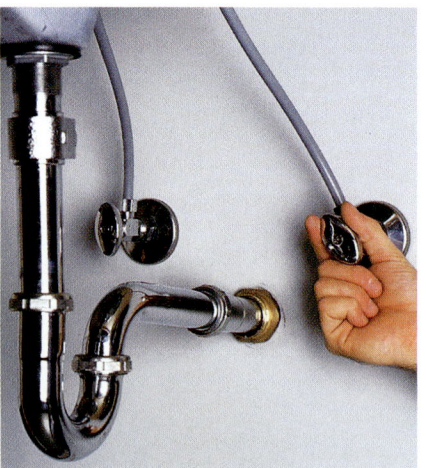

Individual shutoff valves are found on some sinks and most toilets. They are generally located at the supply tubes feeding the fixture. Turn the valve clockwise to stop water flow, then open a faucet or flush the toilet to release water standing in the lines.

Main shutoff valve, located near water meter, can be closed to shut off all water. Open faucets at the highest and lowest points in your home to drain water lines.

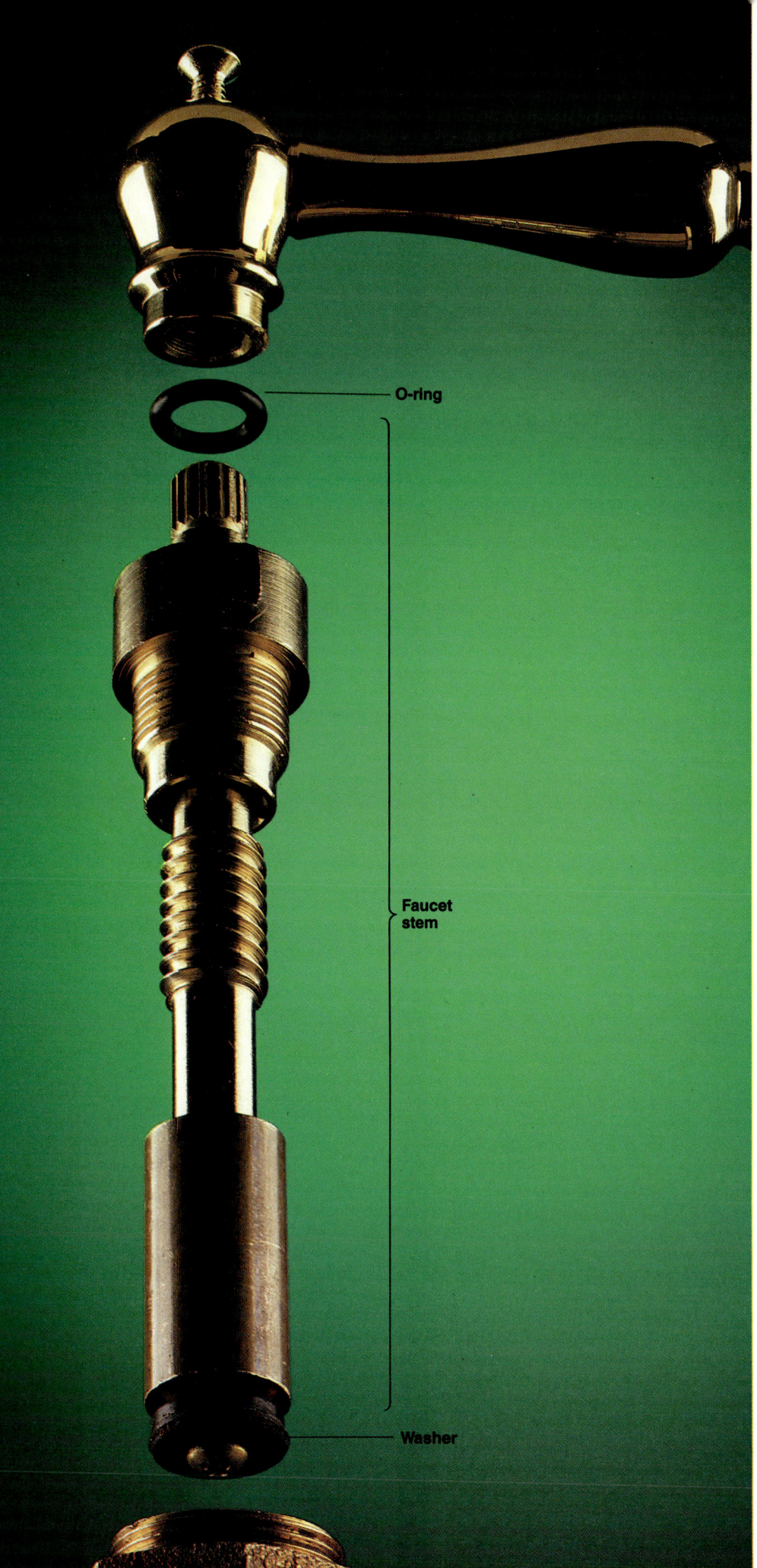

Fixing a Leaky Faucet

When faucets leak, it is usually because the **washers**, **O-rings** or seals are worn or cracked.

Faucets come in dozens of different styles, and the parts may differ widely; but they all have parts that can be replaced when the faucet leaks. When taking a faucet apart, work carefully and pay attention to the arrangement of the parts. Begin by identifying your type of faucet.

Before starting actual work on any fixture, make sure to turn off the water supply.

Before You Start:

Tools & Materials for Ball-type Faucets: channel-type pliers, faucet repair kit(s), utility knife, screwdriver.

Tools & Materials for Disc-type Faucets: allen wrench, screwdriver, cartridge.

Tools & Materials for Sleeve-type Faucets: screwdriver, channel-type pliers, needle-nose pliers, cartridge, O-rings, heatproof grease.

Tools & Materials for Compression (stem and seat) Faucets: screwdriver, adjustable wrench, washers, O-rings or string packing, utility knife, heatproof grease, seat wrench, seat-dressing tool, valve seats.

How to Identify Your Faucet

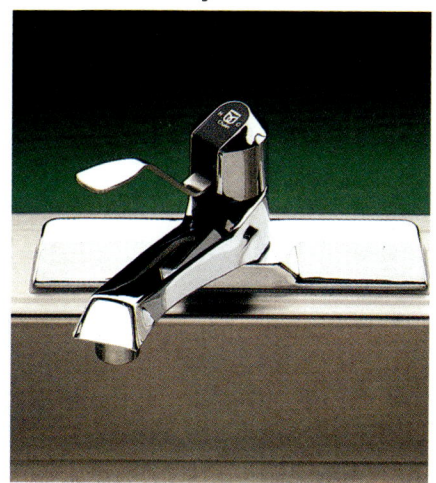

Cartridge faucets, available in many styles, are washerless. They use cartridge inserts that contain all mechanical parts. The handle screw is hidden under an index cap on the collar. The two common types of cartridges are the disc-type and the sleeve-type.
Replacement part for cartridge faucet is a new cartridge. Do not try to replace the cartridge O-rings or seals. To fix a leaky cartridge faucet, see pages 20-21.

Ball-type faucets have a rounded collar on the single-lever handle. Underneath the collar is a dome-shaped cap. The handle is usually held to the faucet by a setscrew located in the collar. Inside, a hollow metal or plastic ball controls the water volume and temperature.
Replacement parts for a ball-type faucet are usually found in two separate repair kits, one containing valve seats and springs, the other including ball, cam and cam washer. Sometimes all these parts are included in a single kit. To fix a leaky ball-type faucet, see page 19.

Compression faucets (stem and seat) on many double-handle sink and tub fixtures have neoprene washers that compress against a valve seat. Index caps on top of faucet handles may conceal the handle screws.
Replacement parts for compression faucet include washer, and O-ring (or packing washer or packing string on older faucets). To fix a leaky compression faucet, see pages 22-23.

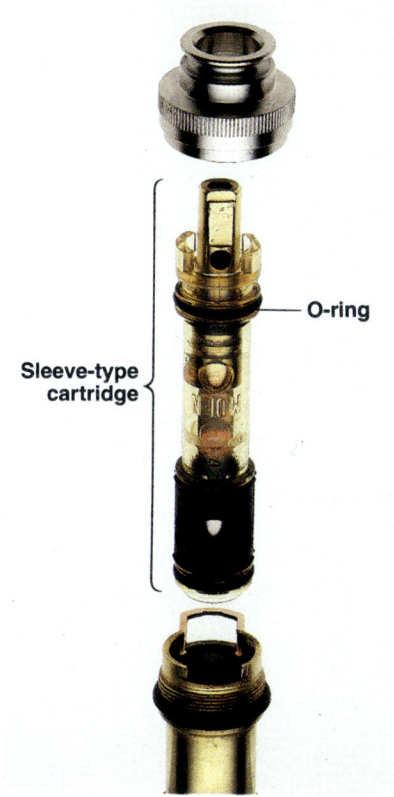

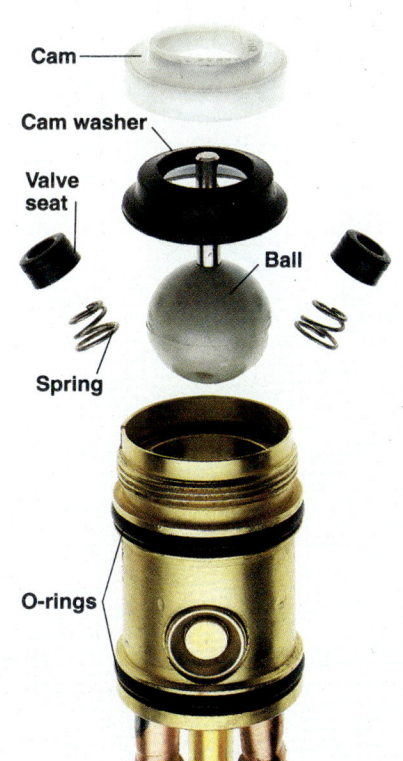

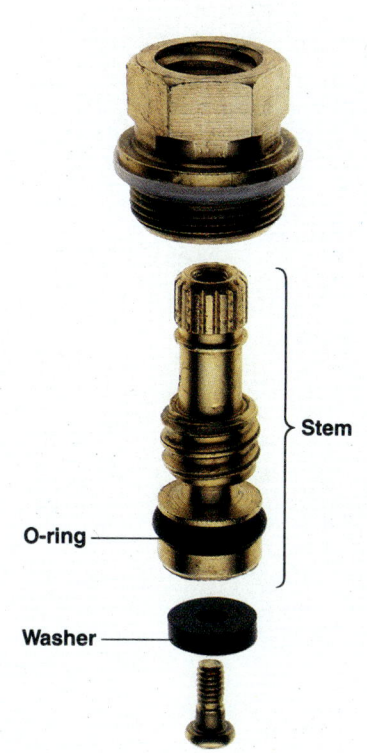

17

Tips & Techniques for Faucets & Spouts

Avoid scratches to chrome by wrapping masking tape around the jaws of pliers or wrench. On double-handle faucets, repair one side at a time to avoid mismatching hot and cold stems.

If the slots on a stem washer are damaged by a screwdriver, deepen the screw slots with a hacksaw. If head of screw breaks, pry out the washer and twist the screw out with a needlenose pliers.

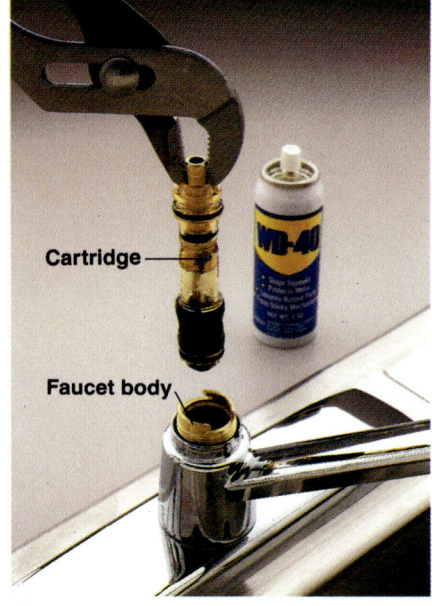

Remove a stubborn cartridge by gripping top of stem with channel-type pliers and lifting with a gentle back-and-forth motion. Applying penetrating oil may help. Be careful not to bend the cartridge or damage the faucet body.

Clean spout attachments if water pressure seems low, or if spray pattern is uneven. Separate all parts and clean off mineral deposits with a brush, then soak all parts overnight in lime-dissolving solution before reassembling. You may choose to replace rather than clean inexpensive aerator and spout attachments.

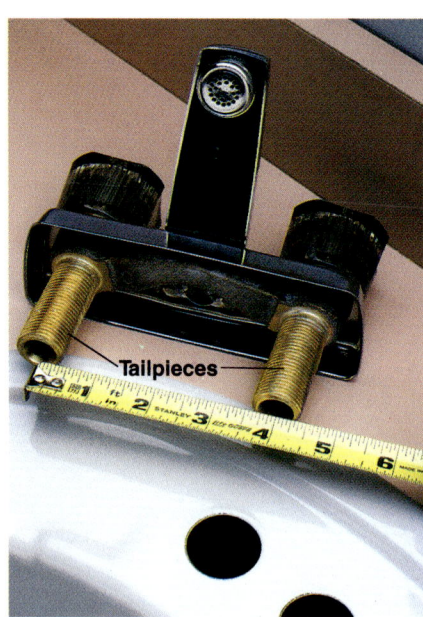

Replace a faucet if it continues to leak. Replacement fixtures come with detailed instructions, but you will need to know measurements to make a proper purchase. Write down on-center measurement between tailpieces, or bring the old faucet along when shopping for a replacement.

How to Fix a Leaky Ball-type Faucet

1 Shut off water supply (page 14). Loosen handle setscrew with an allen wrench (or use the setscrew key included in purchased repair kit). Remove handle to expose adjusting ring located on the cap.

2 Tighten adjusting ring with adjusting wrench included in the repair kit. (On some models, use channel-type pliers to tighten cap.) Reattach the handle, and turn on water. If faucet still leaks, turn off water again and remove the faucet handle.

3 Unscrew cap with channel-type pliers. (Cover jaws of pliers with masking tape or heavy fabric to avoid scratching surface of cap.) Lift out the cam, cam washer and the rotating ball.

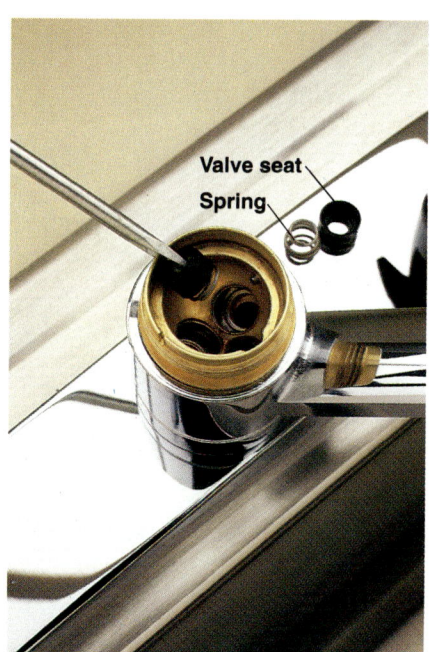

4 Reach into faucet with screwdriver and remove valve seats and springs. Purchase new valve seats, springs, rotating ball, cam and cam washer, available in repair kits.

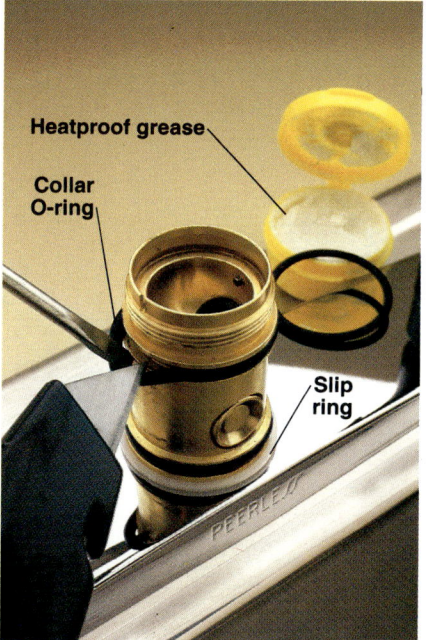

5 Remove spout by twisting upward. Cut old O-rings off with a knife. Coat new O-rings with heatproof grease and install. Reinstall spout, pressing down until collar rests on plastic slip ring.

6 Install new springs and valve seats, and new ball, cam washer and cam. Reassemble faucet.

How to Fix a Leaky Cartridge Faucet (Disc-type)

1 Shut off the water supply (page 14). Pry off the index cap and remove the handle screw underneath. Remove the faucet handle.

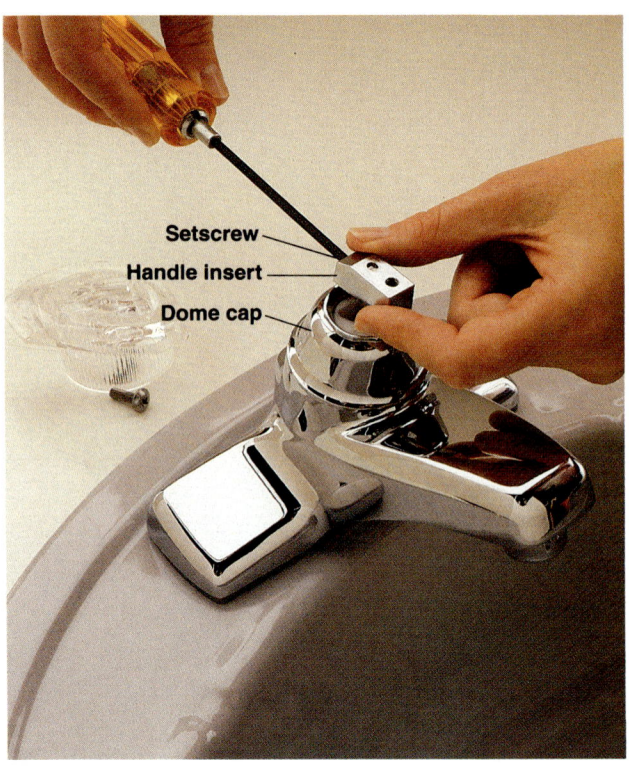

2 Use an allen wrench to loosen the setscrew, then remove the handle insert. Unscrew and lift off the dome cap.

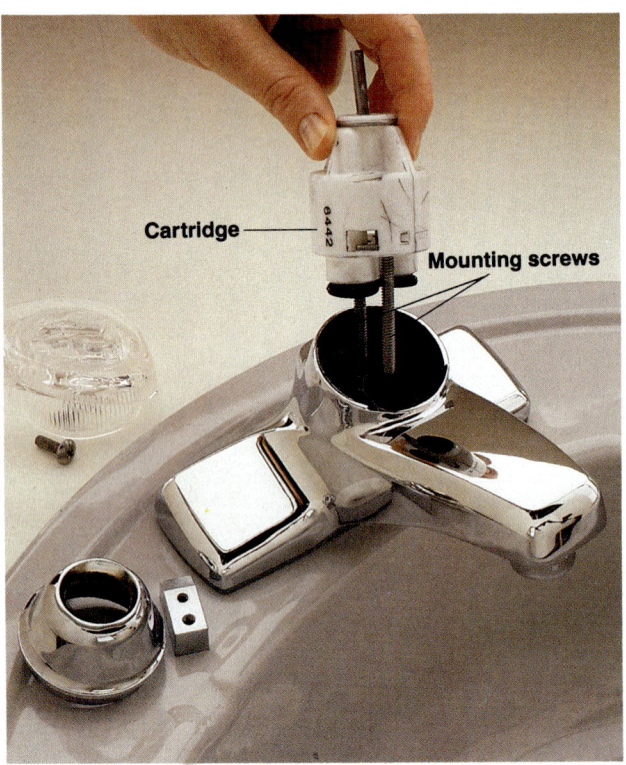

3 Remove mounting screws that hold cartridge in faucet. Lift out cartridge. Purchase a new cartridge that matches the old cartridge.

4 Lower the new cartridge into the faucet body, and replace the mounting screws. Screw on the dome cap. Replace the handle insert, handle and index cap.

How to Fix a Leaky Cartridge Faucet (Sleeve-type)

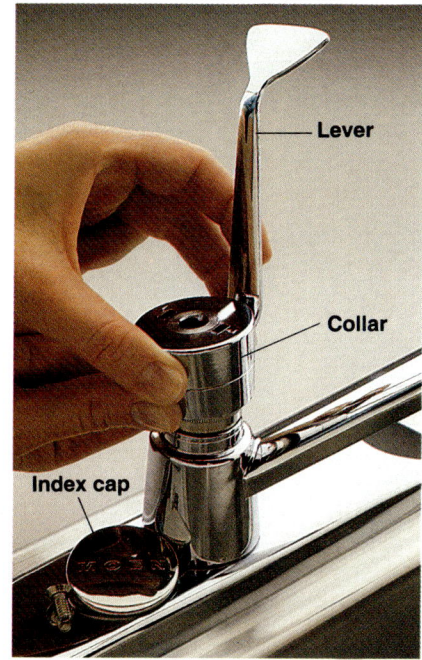

1 Shut off water supply (page 14). Pry off index cap covering collar and remove the handle screw underneath. Lift the lever to the uppermost position to free inner lever from lip of retaining nut. Lift handle off.

2 Remove the retaining nut using channel-type pliers. (On some bathroom faucets, you must also remove a grooved collar under the retaining nut.)

3 Pry the retaining clip from the top of cartridge using needle-nose pliers.

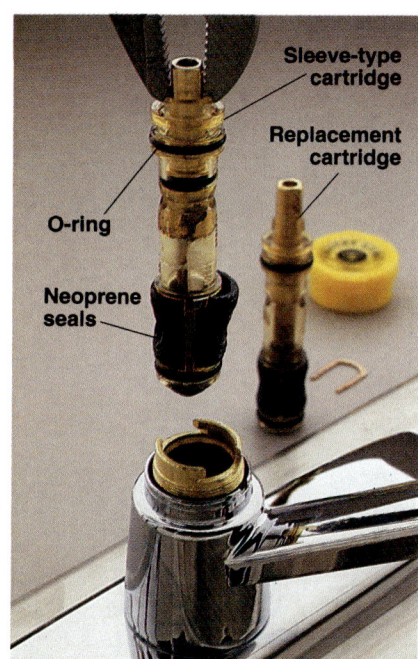

4 Grip top of the cartridge with channel-type pliers. Pull straight up to remove cartridge. Bring old cartridge along when shopping for a replacement. Insert the new cartridge, and install the retaining clip.

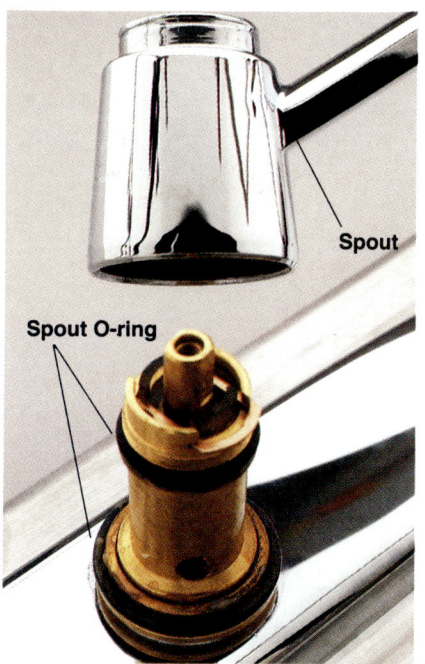

5 Remove spout by pulling up and twisting. Cut off old O-rings using a knife. Spread heatproof grease on new O-rings before installing. Replace spout and retaining nut.

6 Lift handle lever while holding collar tightly. Holding collar at an angle, slip flat edge of inner lever over the lip of retaining nut. Replace the handle screw and index cap.

21

How to Fix a Leaky Compression (Stem and Seat) Faucet

1 Shut off water supply (page 14). Remove the screw holding handle to faucet. (Screw may be hidden under index cap.) Remove handle. If handle sticks, apply penetrating oil and rock handle gently while pulling.

2 Use an adjustable wrench or channel-type pliers to loosen the retaining nut (or packing nut on older faucets). Remove retaining nut by hand, then remove stem from faucet body.

3 Unscrew brass stem screw, and pry out old washer. Replace washer with an exact duplicate. If brass screw shows signs of wear, replace it also. Repair kits include a wide assortment of washers and brass screws.

4 Cut O-ring off stem using a knife. Install duplicate O-ring. Smear heatproof grease on all moving parts, including handle socket. Examine the valve seat (page opposite). If it is pitted, replace or dress valve seat before reassembling faucet.

On older faucets, packing washer or self-forming packing string, found just under the packing nut, is used instead of O-rings. Replace packing washer; or hold stem with packing nut facing you, and wrap 5 or 6 loops of packing string clockwise around stem under packing nut.

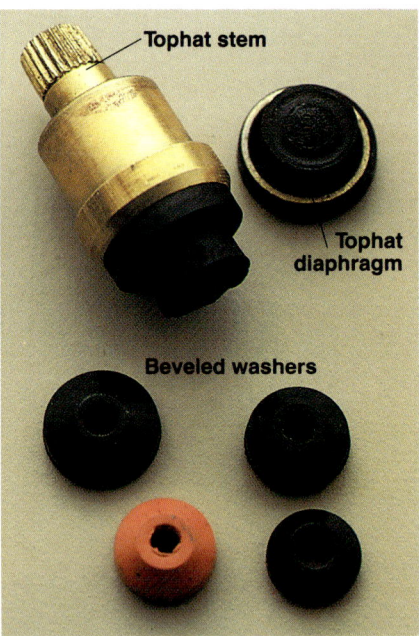

Washer variations: A tophat stem faucet uses a tophat-shaped diaphragm. Simply pop a new diaphragm washer over the stem tip to fix leaks. A reverse-pressure stem uses a beveled washer that fits with beveled side facing the stem body.

How to Remove a Wall-mounted Compression Faucet

1 For double-handle compression faucets mounted on the wall, remove handle using the same method as for sink faucets (page opposite). Remove escutcheon from fitting. Escutcheon may be held with setscrew.

2 Remove bonnet nut using reversible ratchet and deep socket. (Trim back wall tile and chip out plaster or concrete around nut, if necessary.) If nut sticks, apply penetrating oil and wait 15 minutes.

3 Remove and replace stem washer. Remove and replace old O-ring, old packing washer or packing string. Lubricate stem lightly with heatproof grease, then reassemble faucet.

How to Replace or Dress a Worn Valve Seat

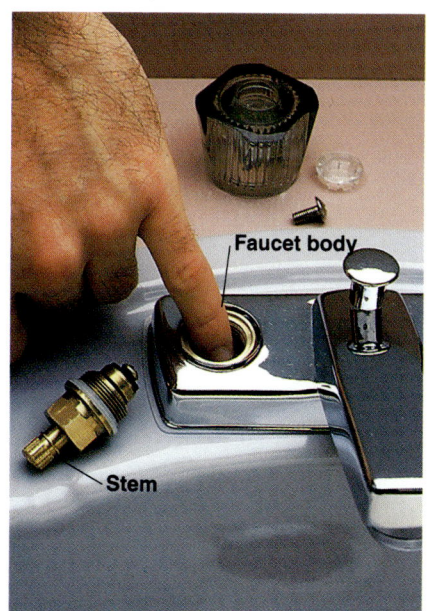

1 Continuing leaks could mean that a brass valve seat inside the faucet body is damaged. Remove faucet stem and feel valve seat with a fingertip. If rough, replace the seat, or resurface it with a seat-dressing tool (right).

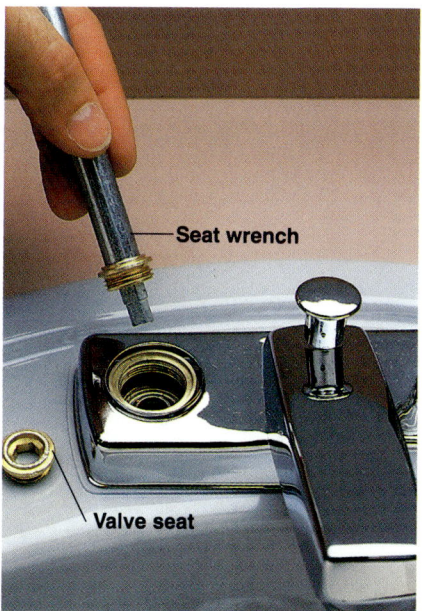

2 Remove a deteriorated valve seat using seat wrench. Select end of wrench that fits valve seat and insert into faucet. Turn counterclockwise to remove. Use wrench to insert new seat. If the seat cannot be removed, resurface using a seat-dressing tool (right).

To dress (resurface) a valve seat, select a guide disc to fit faucet. Attach disc to dressing tool and insert through retaining nut. Tighten retaining nut lightly into faucet. Press tool down lightly and turn grinder clockwise. Seat is dressed when tool turns easily.

All **tank toilets** work the same way. When you push the **handle (1)**, the **trip lever (2)** attached to the lift chain or **lift wires (3)** raises the **tank ball (4)** or flapper at the bottom of the tank (water closet). Fresh water rushes down into the toilet bowl. As the water level in the water closet drops, a **float ball (5)** or float cup opens the **ballcock (6)** to let in fresh water.

Fixing a Running Toilet

Continuously running water in a toilet occurs when the water intake valve (ballcock) does not shut off the fresh water at the end of the flush cycle. This problem can be caused by a **float device** that is out of adjustment, by a faulty **ballcock**, or by a defective **flapper** or **tank ball**.

> **Before You Start:**
>
> Tools & Materials: emery paper, ballcock repair kit, screwdrivers.

Toilet Flush Adjustment

If toilet flushes too slowly, straighten the lift wire or chain or move the chain to a different hole in the trip lever. You may need to install a longer lift chain. If toilet will not flush at all, or will not flush unless handle is held down, hook the lift chain or wire through a trip lever hole that is closer to the handle.

24

When the water closet is empty, the tank ball (1) or flapper falls back into place to seal the tank. Incoming water from the **ballcock (2)** refills the water closet, while the **refill tube (3)** sends a stream of fresh water down the **overflow tube (4)** to restore the water level in the toilet bowl. As the water closet reaches full capacity, the **float rod (5)** attached to the **float ball (6)** pivots to close the ballcock.

How to Identify the Problem

Remove tank lid and look inside the water closet. If water is running into overflow tube, then adjust float device (page 26). If water continues to run after adjustment, then repair the ballcock (page 27).

If water does not run over lip of overflow tube, then repair the flapper or tank ball (page 26).

How to Adjust a Float Device

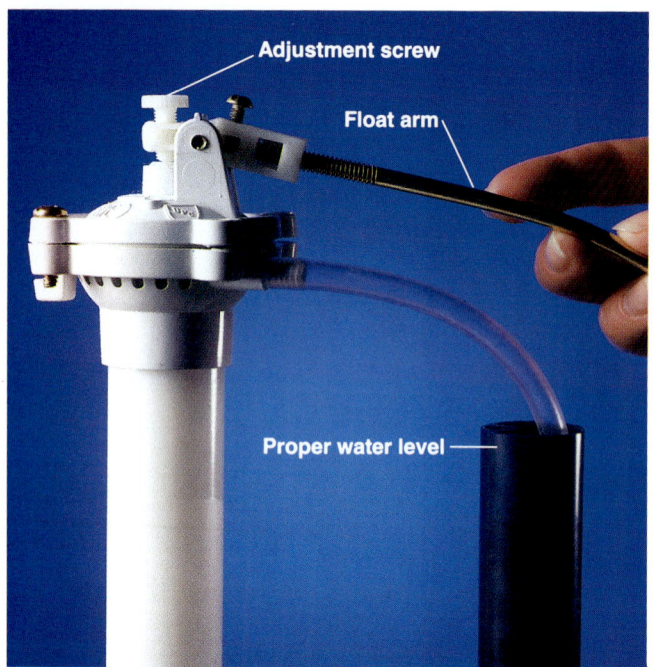
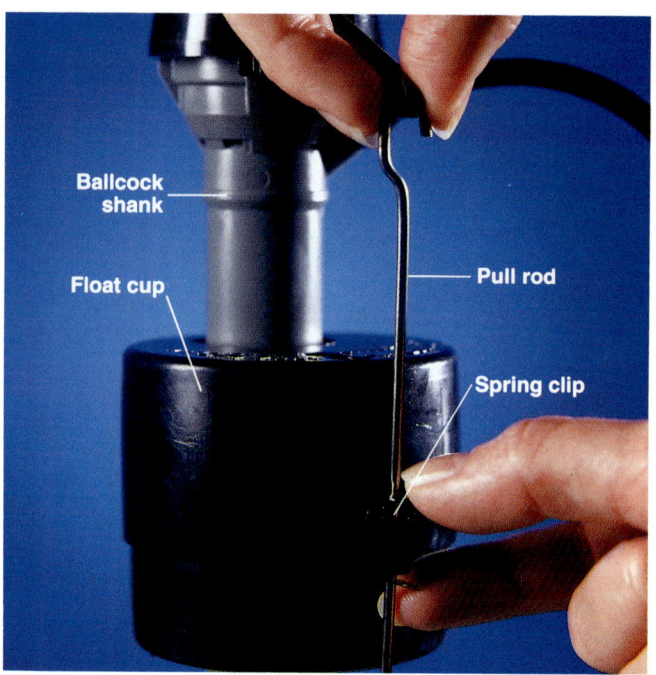

Toilets with float balls. Bend float arm down slightly. Water level in water closet should reach a point about ½ inch below edge of overflow tube. Most, but not all, ballcocks also have adjustment screws for small water-level adjustments. Replace a float ball that contains water. Ball should not touch walls of water closet.

Toilets with float cups. Pinch the spring clip attached to the pull rod and adjust the position of the cup on the ballcock shank. Adjust the cup downward to lower the water level in the water closet.

How to Fix a Leaky Tank Ball or Flapper

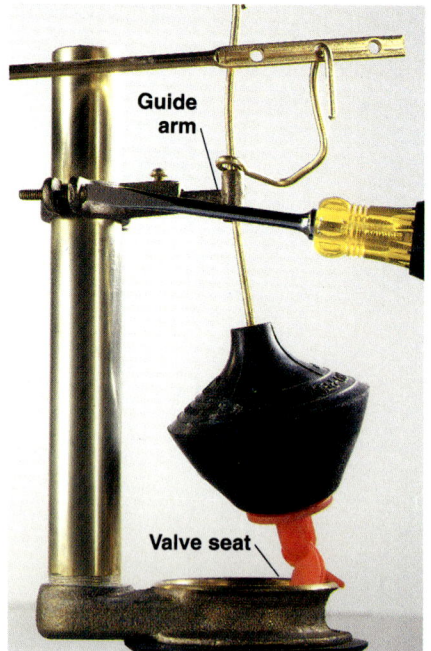
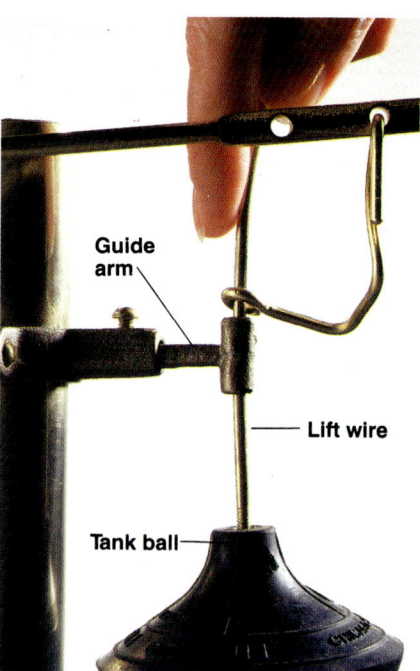

1 Shut off water supply (page 14) and flush to empty water closet. Lift tank ball or unhook flapper. Gently scrub inside of valve seat and rim with emery paper.

2 Line up the tank ball. Loosen the screws holding guide arm, and position the arm directly over the valve seat. Replace a flapper or tank ball that is soft or cracked.

3 Straighten vertical lift wire on tank ball assembly. Ball should rise and fall smoothly when lever is tripped. Turn on water to refill tank, and test by flushing.

How to Fix a Leaky Plunger Valve Ballcock

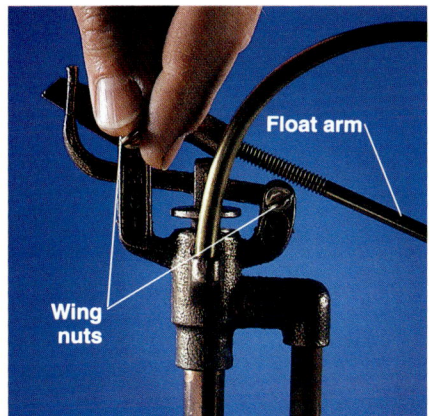
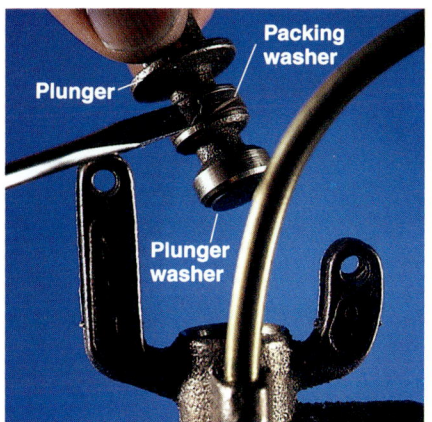

1 Shut off water supply (page 14) and flush to empty water closet. Remove wing nuts on ballcock. Slip the float arm out.

2 Pull up on plunger to remove it. Pry out old washer. (Remove stem screw, if necessary.) Pry out slotted packing washer or O-ring.

3 Replace washers. Clean sediment from inside of ballcock, and reassemble.

How to Fix a Leaky Diaphragm Ballcock

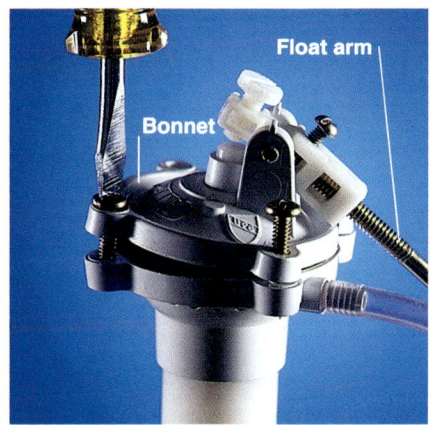
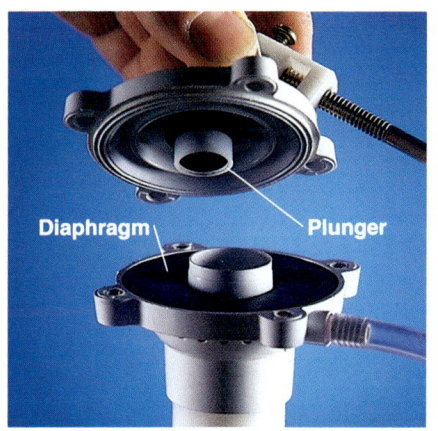
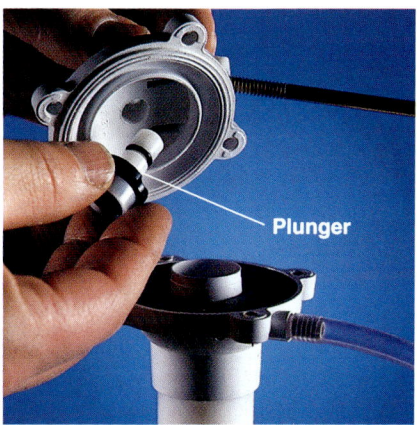

1 Shut off water supply (page 14) and flush to empty water closet. Remove screws from bonnet.

2 Lift off ballcock float arm with bonnet attached. Check diaphragm and valve plunger for wear.

3 Replace parts that are stiff or cracked. If assembly is too worn, replace entire ballcock.

How to Fix a Leaky Float Cup Assembly

1 Shut off water supply (page 14) and flush to empty water closet. Remove cap.

2 Push down on shaft and turn to left to remove bonnet. Examine inside of valve, and clean out any sediment.

3 Replace valve seal. If assembly is too worn, replace the entire ballcock.

Opening a Clogged Drain

Drains clog when waste collects in the drain pipes, slowing or blocking the route to the sewer. Your drain system contains several built-in access points for dealing with clogs.

Each fixture in your plumbing system contains a safety device known as a trap, a curved section of pipe. If only one drain is blocked, use a plunger or expansion nozzle on the drain (page opposite).

Drains for more than one fixture sometimes feed into the same branch drain. The branch drain feeds into a vertical pipe known as a soil stack. If two or more drains are blocked, clear the branch drain using a drain auger (page 30).

At the bottom of the soil stack, the pipe takes a gradual 90° turn to join the main drain. If a floor drain backs up, use chemical root remover in main drain (page 31), or call a professional.

Before You Start:

Tools & Materials: drain plunger, screwdrivers, expansion nozzle, channel-type pliers, wire brush, pipe wrench, drain auger, rubber gloves, pail, copper sulfate root remover, heat-proof grease, lime-dissolving solution.

Tip: Be careful when using chemical drain cleaners. They generate heat that can damage pipes, and they may pit enamel surfaces. Never pour drain cleaners into standing water, and never use plunger when standing water contains chemicals. Remember to wear eye protection.

How to Use a Drain Plunger

1 Remove any drain stopper. On some drains, unscrew the retaining nut holding the ball pivot to eye of pop-up stopper (page 32). Some pop-up stoppers lift out; others turn counterclockwise.

2 Stuff a wet rag in the overflow opening. Place plunger cup over drain; run enough water to cover cup. Move plunger down and up several times to force water through drain, keeping cup sealed over drain.

On tubs with trip-lever or pop-up drain stoppers, remove screws on overflow plate and carefully pull lift assembly out of overflow opening. Remove stopper on pop-up assembly. Plug the overflow opening with wet rag before plunging drain.

How to Use an Expansion Nozzle

An expansion nozzle (blow bag) may be useful on small local clogs on sink drains with removable stoppers. Attach nozzle to garden hose, and attach hose to faucet. Remove stopper. Insert hose into drain. When hose is turned on, nozzle expands to fill drain pipe, then releases water in spurts to clear clogs.

A floor or shower drain can also be cleared using the expansion nozzle. After clearing any drain with an expansion nozzle, turn water off and wait for nozzle to empty before removing it.

How to Open a Drain Trap Bend

1 Place pail under trap to catch water and debris. Wear rubber gloves if chemical drain cleaner has been used. Loosen slip nuts on trap bend with channel-type pliers, then remove nuts by hand and slide away from connections. Pull trap bend off.

2 Dump out debris. Scrub inside of bend with brush. Replace a corroded bend (page opposite). Reassemble trap; tighten nuts with channel-type pliers, but do not overtighten. Test drain by running water. If drain leaks, tighten nuts another ¼ turn.

How to Open a Clogged Branch Drain (Chrome-plated brass pipe shown)

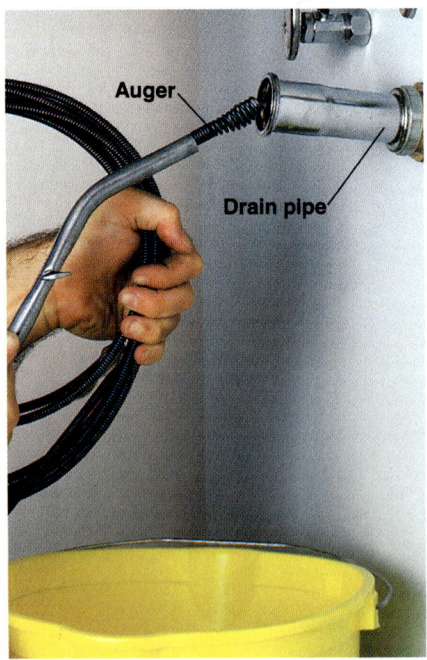
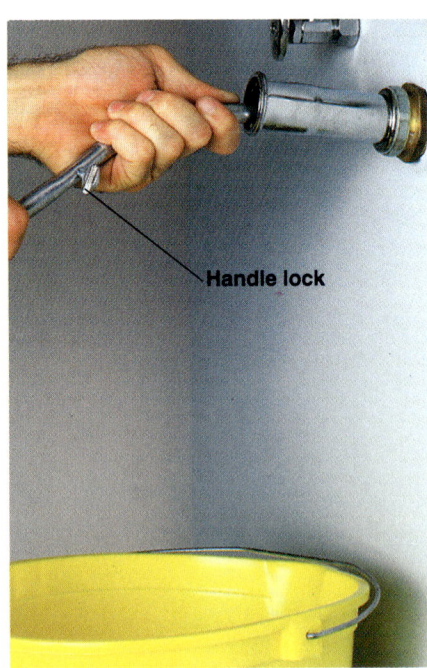

1 Place pail under trap bend and arm. Remove bend (above). Use channel-type pliers or pipe wrench to loosen the slip nut that holds trap arm to drain pipe.

2 Remove nut by hand and slide away from connection. Remove arm. Feed coil of the drain auger into drain pipe until clog is reached. Tighten the wing screw to lock auger handle.

3 Rotate auger clockwise. Feed more coil and continue rotating as clog breaks up. When coil moves freely, remove auger while rotating handle. Reassemble drain, then plunge drain opening vigorously and flush with water.

How to Install a Drain Trap (PVC plastic pipe shown)

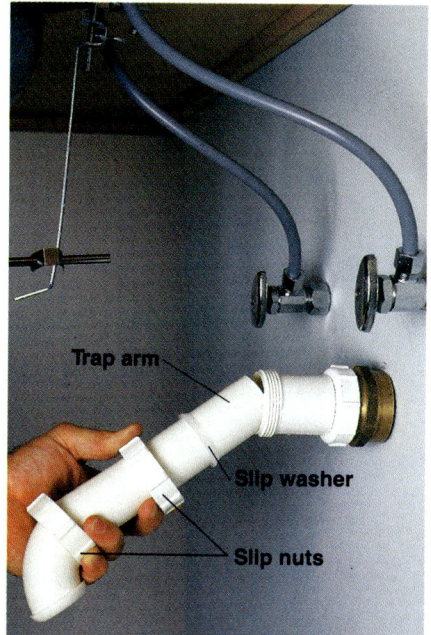 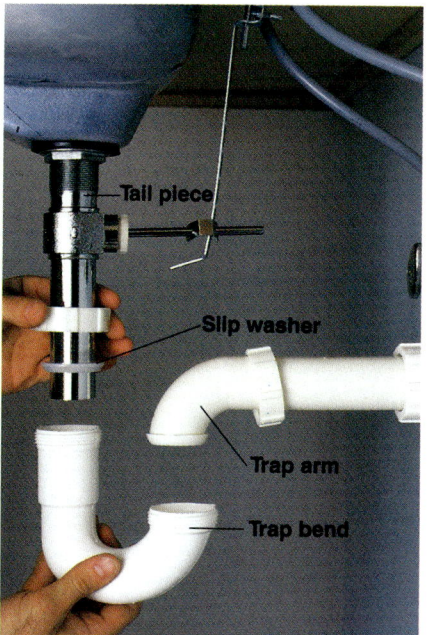 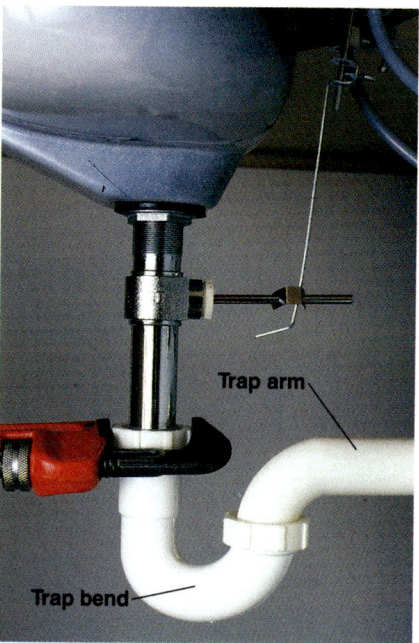

1 Slide fittings onto trap arm in following order: slip nut (threads first), another slip nut (threads last), and slip washer (beveled-side last). Push trap arm about 1½ inches into drain pipe. Slide washer onto drain opening and tighten slip nut over it by hand.

2 Slide slip nut onto tailpiece (threads down), then a washer (beveled-side down). Push long end of trap bend onto tailpiece and slide up until short end is aligned with trap arm. Slip the washer and nut down the tailpiece and tighten onto bend by hand.

3 Move position of trap arm in wall to align it with short end of trap bend. Tighten all nuts with channel-type pliers or a pipe wrench, but do not overtighten. Test drain by running water. If the drain leaks, tighten the slip nuts another ¼ turn.

How to Remove Tree Roots from a Main Drain

1 Unscrew main cleanout plug with a pipe wrench. With a corroded plug, drill holes in plug, and break it apart with a ball peen hammer. Install a new plug after clearing the drain.

2 Pour about 2 cups copper sulfate root remover into main cleanout. Replace main cleanout plug. Allow remover to work overnight before running water or flushing toilet. Roots are killed by crystals, then are washed away.

How to Clean & Adjust a Tub Stopper Assembly

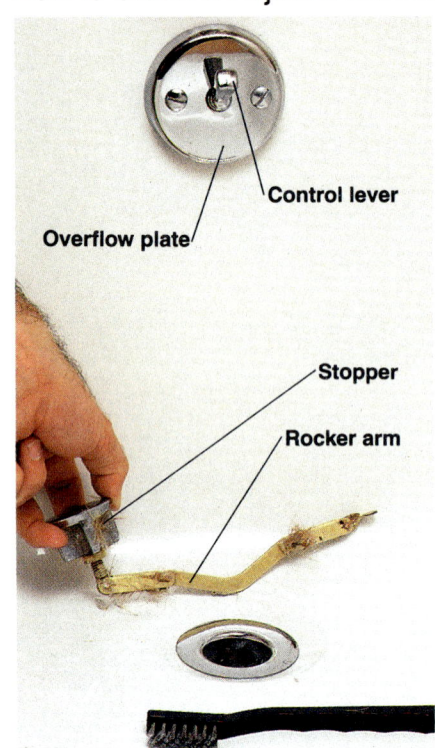  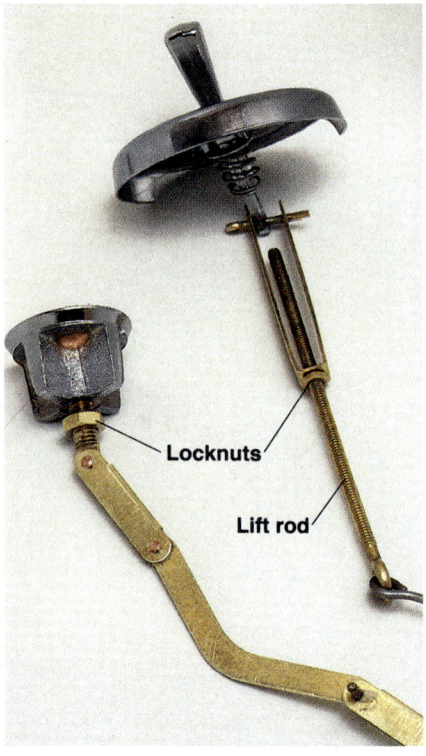

1 Turn control lever on pop-up stopper to open position. Pull up stopper and carefully pull rocker arm from drain. Clean debris from stopper. Remove screws on the overflow plate.

2 Remove plate and lift assembly from the overflow tube. Clean debris from lift assembly with a stiff brush. Remove corrosion with lime-dissolving solution or vinegar. Lubricate all parts with heatproof grease.

3 Locknuts allow adjustment of stopper position. If tub drain leaks when stopper is closed, then loosen stopper locknut and screw stopper down. If tub drains too slowly, then screw stopper up. Make larger adjustments by changing position of lift rod.

How to Fix a Pop-up Sink Drain Stopper

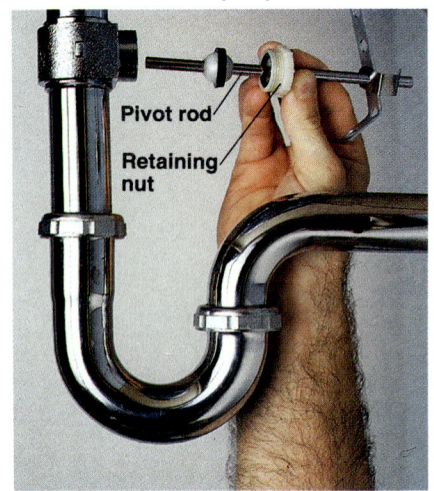 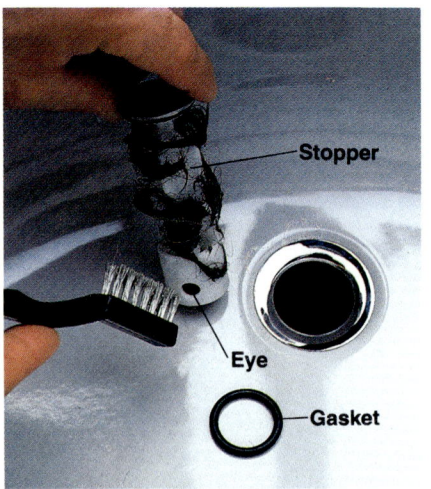 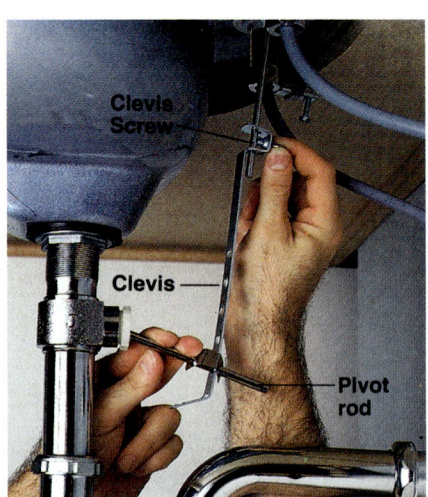

1 Raise stopper to open position. Unscrew retaining nut below sink, then pull pivot rod out of drain body to release plug. Remove stopper by rotating counterclockwise and lifting.

2 Clean debris from stopper. Pry off any worn gasket and install replacement. Return stopper to drain. If stopper has an eye, make sure eye aligns with pivot rod. Insert pivot rod below sink and tighten retaining nut.

3 If sink does not drain properly, loosen clevis screw below sink. Pull pivot rod down, and retighten clevis screw. If plug does not operate smoothly, move pivot rod to a higher hole in clevis.

Opening a Clogged Toilet

Toilet clogs usually occur in the sharp, narrow bends of the built-in **trap**. The location of the trap depends on the style of toilet. In the common jet toilet, the bowl empties through an **outlet** at the rear of the bowl.

Begin repair by bailing out water in bowl. While wearing a rubber glove, reach into the outlet opening as far as possible to check for foreign objects. If you can't reach the clog this way, continue with the directions below.

Before You Start:

Tools & Materials: plunger, closet auger, rubber glove.

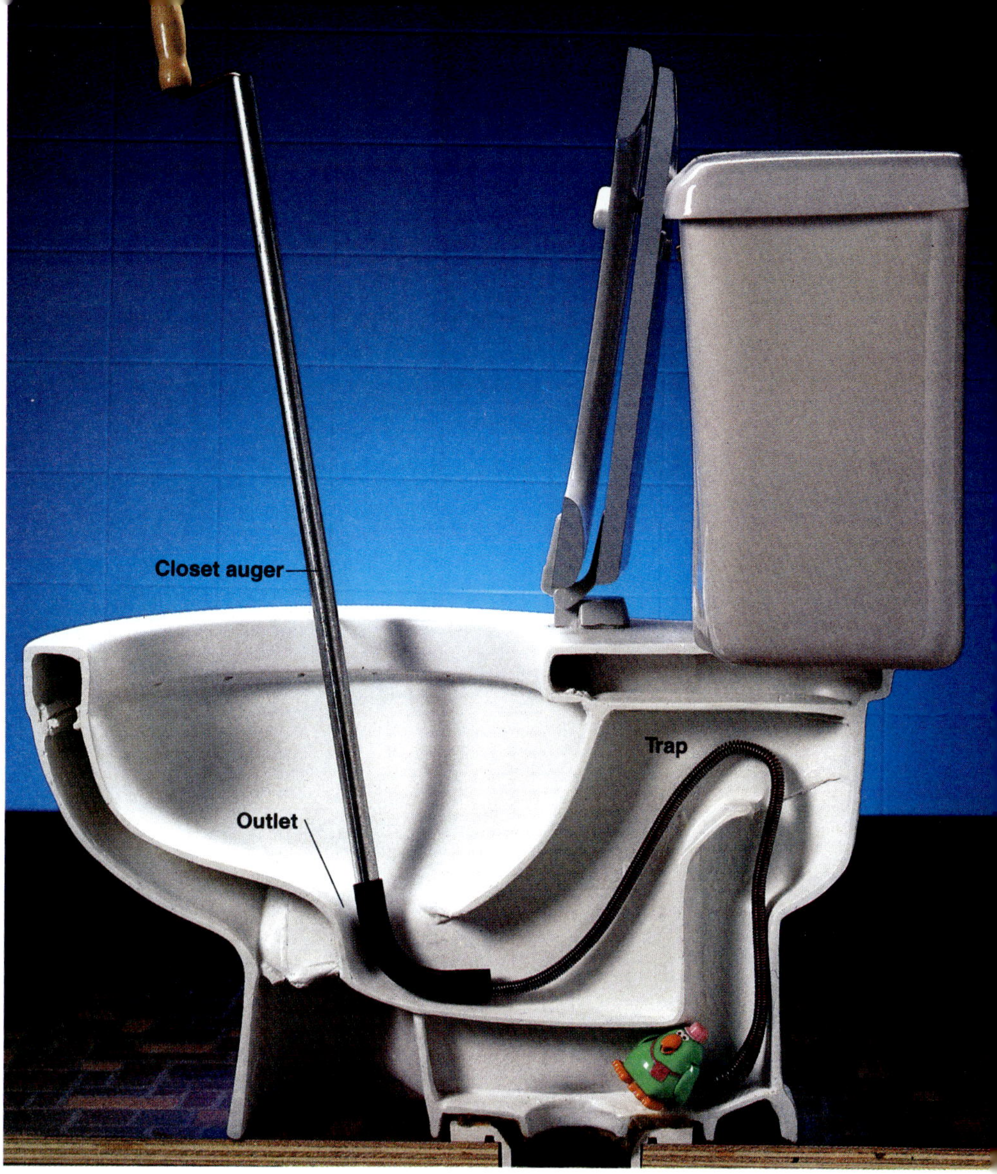

How to Open a Clogged Toilet with a Plunger

Place cup of plunger over outlet opening. (Flanged plunger works best on toilets.) Pour enough water into bowl to cover rubber cup. Plunge down and up rapidly. Pour a bucket of water into the bowl. If water passes through, flush toilet several times to wash debris through drain.

How to Open Clogged Toilet with an Auger

Use a closet auger designed specifically for clearing toilet clogs. Insert the curved rubber sleeve into the outlet opening and crank the handle to work the coil into the toilet trap. When the tip bites into the clog, carefully extract the debris, or move the auger coil back and forth to break up the clog.

Electrical

Basic Electrical Know-how

Electricity flows through your home's wiring system much like water flowing through a network of hoses. Each electrical circuit contains a "hot" wire, usually colored black, which moves electricity outward from the main service panel. A second "neutral" wire, usually white, carries current back to the source.

Making electrical repairs usually means replacing plugs, outlets, switches or light fixtures. Electrical repairs are completely safe as long as you shut off the power to the wires you touch.

If an appliance is not working, check to see if the cord is plugged into an outlet. Appliance manufacturers report that in more than half of all service calls, the problem is an unplugged appliance.

Test for electricity with an inexpensive neon circuit tester (left) before touching any wires. If circuit tester lights, it means that the wires are live and not safe to touch. When testing switched lights or appliances, make sure the switch is in the ON position. Each electrical repair in this book describes a quick way to test for electricity before beginning work.

How to Find the Main Service Panel

Entry pipe

1 Look for the service wires on the outside of the home. Service wires pass through the electrical meter, usually found on an exterior wall. Close to the meter, a metal pipe called a service entry brings the wires through the outside wall and into the home. Find the main service panel by tracing the service entry pipe through the wall into your basement or utility room.

Combination tool

Needlenose pliers

Insulated screwdriver

Neon circuit tester

Fuse puller

Continuity tester

Wire nuts

Tools for Electrical Repair

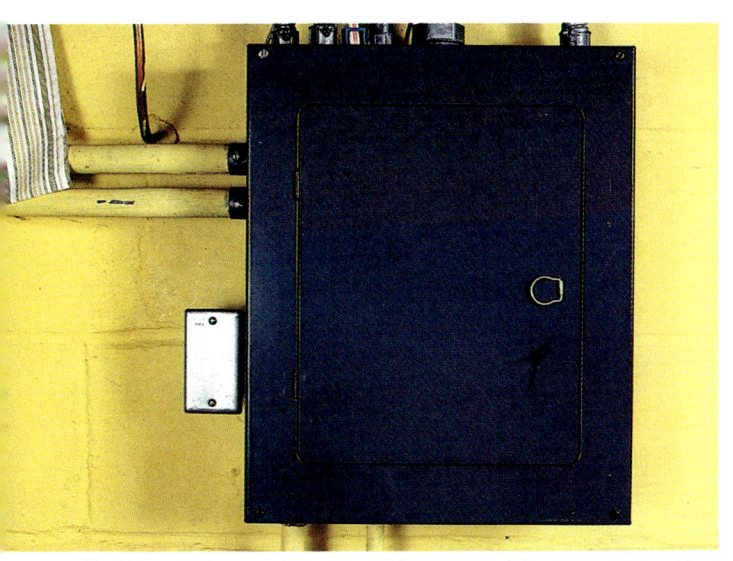

2 The main service panel is a metal box attached to the entry pipe. The panel divides the electricity into circuits, each carrying power to a part of your home. In newer systems, each circuit is controlled by a circuit breaker. Older systems use screw-in plug fuses. The main breaker or fuse makes it possible to turn off all power at once.

Sub panel

A sub panel, sometimes found near the main service panel, feeds directly off the main service panel to provide power to appliance circuits, or to a garage or other outbuilding. Shutting off the main fuse or breaker in the main service panel also shuts off power to the sub panel.

37

Electrical Safety

Avoid shock when making electrical repairs by turning off the power at the main service panel, then testing the wires before you touch them.

Electricity is dangerous only if it flows outside the established wiring system. By nature, electricity seeks to return to earth along the easiest path. If power "leaks" and finds a path outside the circuit wires, shock or fire can occur.

To prevent this type of power leak — known as a **short circuit** — your electrical network depends on a **ground system**. If circuit wires fail, the ground system provides a controlled route for electricity to follow. In newer wiring, bare copper or insulated green wires run through the system. These are ground wires. When making electrical repairs, always reconnect the ground wires. Before replacing an older 2-prong outlet receptacle with a new 3-prong model, always check the system to see if it is grounded (page opposite).

If a circuit breaker trips, move appliances to other circuits, then switch lever of tripped breaker fully to OFF, then to ON. **If a fuse blows,** it means that lights and appliances are drawing more power than the circuit can safely handle. Plug appliances into other circuits, then install a duplicate fuse. If a fuse or breaker blows immediately after being replaced or reset, there may be a short circuit. Call an electrician immediately.

How to Shut Off Electricity Before Making Repairs

Circuit breakers control current load in newer systems. Identify breaker controlling wires you will touch. Switch breaker to OFF. **Test wires with circuit tester** before beginning repair.

Fuses control current load in older wiring systems. Identify the fuse controlling wires you will touch. **Touching insulated rim only,** unscrew fuse and set aside. **Test wires with circuit tester** before beginning repair.

Cartridge fuses protect circuits for larger appliances. **Use one hand only** to open panel and handle fuses. If fuse is housed in a block, grip handle of block and pull. Remove fuse from clips using fuse puller.

Electrical Safety Tips

Read markings on old outlet and switches before buying replacements. Choose replacements with the same voltage and amp ratings. If you have aluminum wiring, or if the old outlet or switch is marked CO/ALR, select a similar replacement.

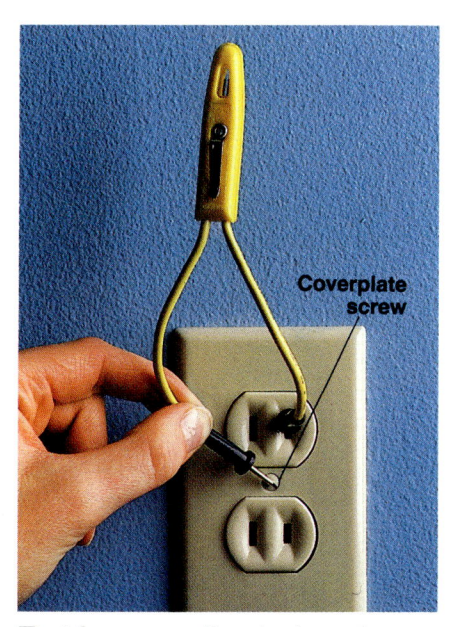

Test for grounding by inserting one probe of neon circuit tester in a vertical slot. Touch other probe to metal coverplate screw. Repeat test with other vertical slot. If tester lights, outlet is grounded, and a new 3-slot receptacle can be installed (page 46).

Install GFCI (ground-fault circuit interrupter) whenever replacing a receptacle near water or plumbing, or outside. A GFCI detects changes in current flow and quickly shuts off electricity in outlet before shock can occur. Install GFCI receptacles in laundry rooms, bathrooms, kitchen or outdoor outlets.

Three-prong plugs should be used only in a properly grounded outlet. If using a 3-prong adapter, test to make sure it is grounded. Do not alter the plug to fit a 2-slot receptacle.

Polarized plugs use prongs of different width to maintain proper circuit continuity and protect against shock. If you have a receptacle that will not accept polarized plugs, do not alter the plugs to fit the outlet. Install a new receptacle (page 46) after testing outlet for grounding.

Protect children against the possibility of electrical shock. Place tight protective caps in any receptacles that are not being used.

39

Tips & Techniques for Electrical Repairs

Dry your hands before plugging in or unplugging appliances. Water conducts electricity and increases the possibility of shock.

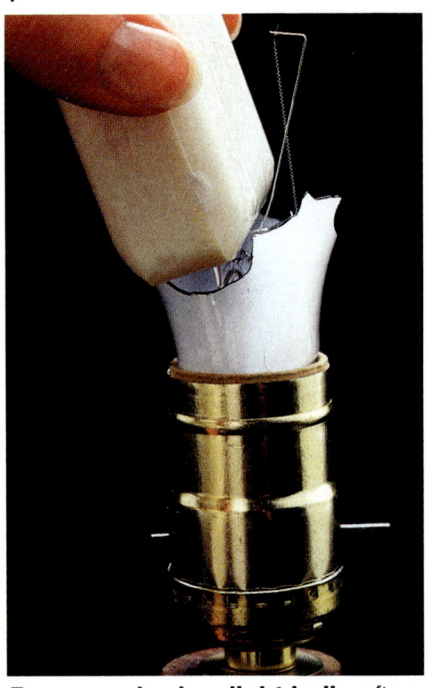

Remove a broken light bulb, after turning off electricity or unplugging lamp, by inserting a bar of soap, then turning counterclockwise. Discard soap. Or use needlenose pliers to grip filament or metal base of bulb.

Mark the wires with small tabs of masking tape before disconnecting an old receptacle or switch. Attach wires to new receptacle or switch using tape marks as a guide.

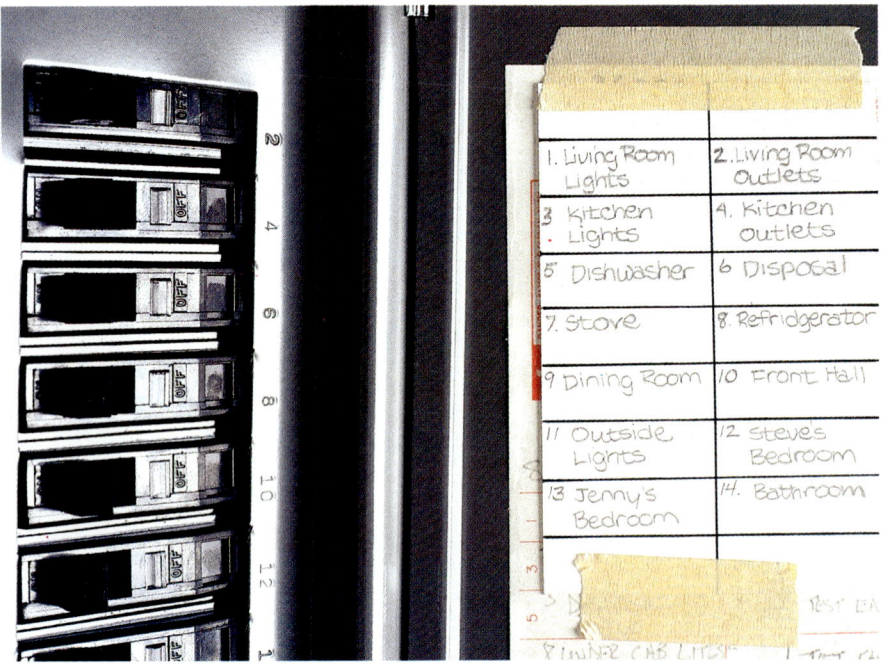

A circuit map can simplify repairs. Shut off power to one circuit at a time (page 38). For each circuit, check throughout the house and make a list of which outlets, appliances and lights do not carry power. Tape a description of the circuits on the door of the service panel. Write the circuit number on the back of outlet and switch coverplates.

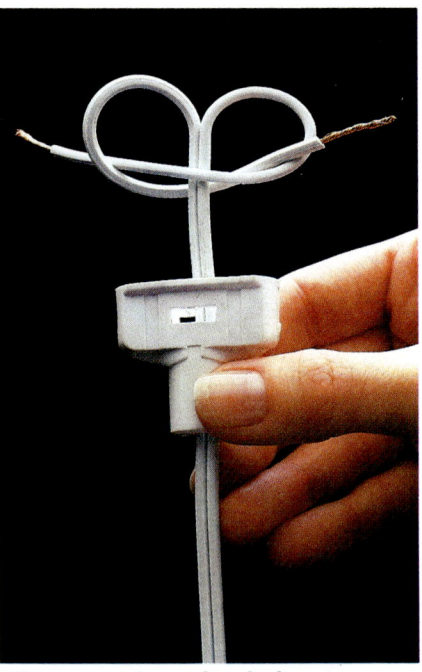

Tie an underwriter's knot as shown when replacing an electrical plug or cord, if there is space in the plug body. This prevents the wires from being pulled from the plug.

How to Make Electrical Connections

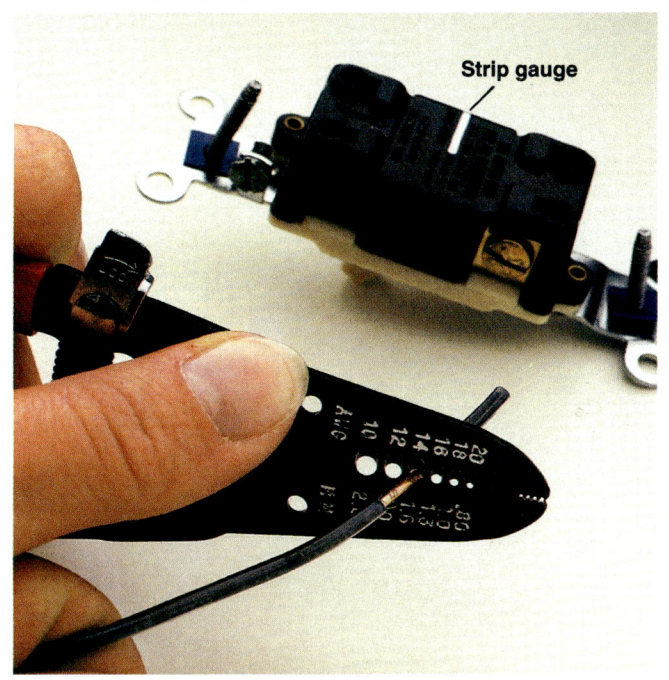

Use a combination tool to strip wire. Strip gauge on back of outlet or switch shows length of stripped wire needed. Insert insulated end of wire into proper hole of combination tool. Press jaws together, then use the thumb to lever tool sideways to strip off insulation.

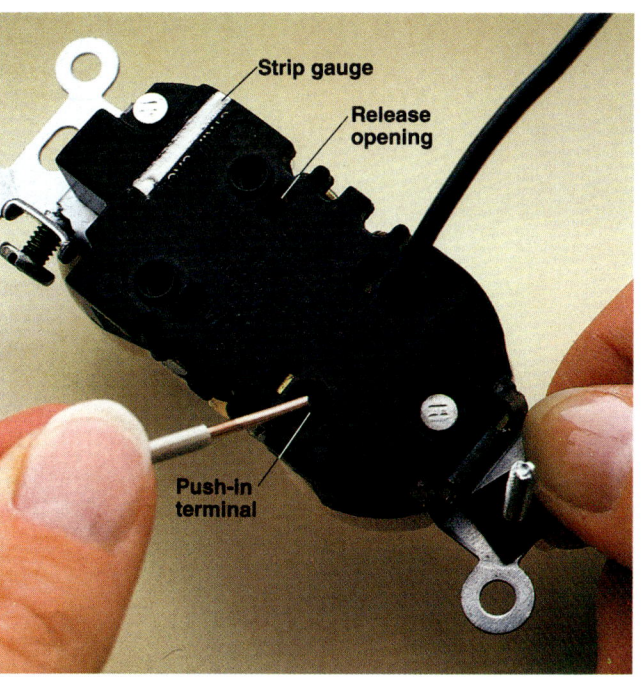

Make quick connections in outlets and switches by stripping wire to length indicated by strip gauge. Press bare wires into push-in terminals. On receptacles, black wire fits into hole nearest darker screw. To release connections, push a nail or tip of small screwdriver into release opening next to wire.

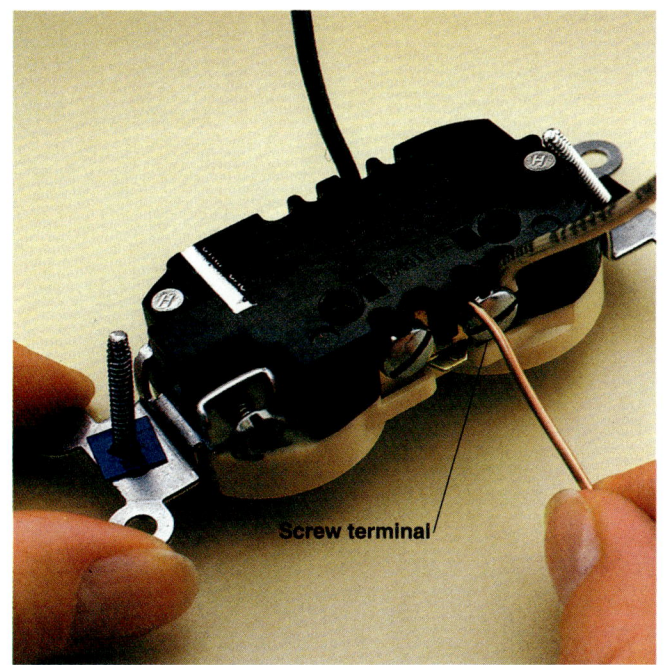

Make a screw terminal connection by stripping about 2 inches of insulation from wire. Wrap wire clockwise around screw terminal so that insulation is flush against screw. To make a neat connection, tighten screw firmly, then bend bare wire back and forth until excess breaks off.

Make wire nut connection by stripping off about 5/8 inch of insulation from wire. Use a wire nut that fits size and number of wires to be connected. Hold parallel copper ends together, and screw on wire nut clockwise until bare wires are covered and connection is tight. Tug slightly on wires to check connection.

Replacing a Cord Plug

Replace an electrical cord plug whenever you notice bent or loose prongs, a cracked or damaged casing, a missing insulating faceplate; or if you notice exposed wires or worn insulation in the cord near the plug.

Several types of replacement plugs are available for lamp and appliance cords. Flat-cord plugs, used on light-duty appliances, contain two screw terminals. A quick-fix option for flat-cord repairs is a quick-connect plug. Round-cord plugs are used with larger cords, including those containing a third, grounding wire. Always choose a replacement that is similar to the defective plug.

Before You Start:

Tools & Materials: replacement plug, combination tool, needlenose pliers, screwdriver.

How to Replace a Flat-cord Plug

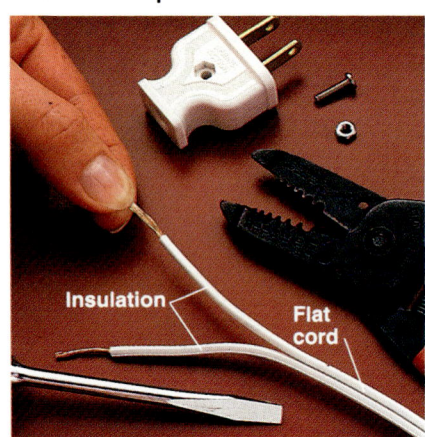

1 Cut old plug from cord using combination tool. Separate flat-cord wires by pulling the two halves apart. Strip ¾ inch of insulation on each wire using combination tool.

2 Remove casing cover. Twist loose strands of bare copper wire together. Hook copper wires clockwise around screw terminals and tighten securely.

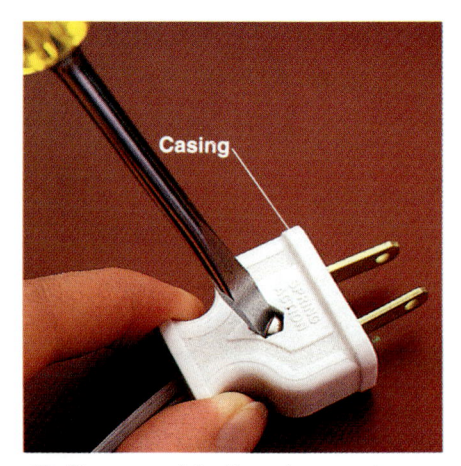

3 Reassemble the plug casing. Replace insulating faceplate, if plug uses one.

How to Install a Quick-connect Plug

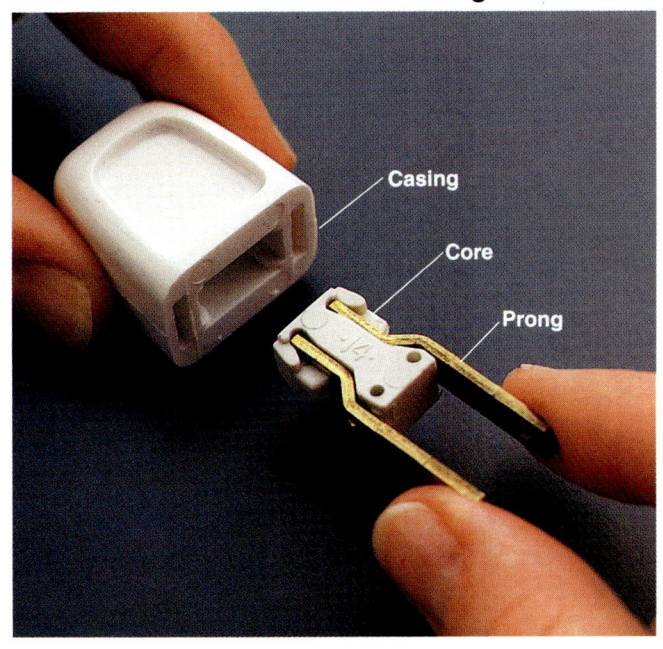

1 Squeeze prongs of new quick-connect plug together slightly and pull plug core from casing. Cut old plug from flat-cord wire using combination tool, leaving a clean-cut end.

2 Feed unstripped flat-cord wire through rear of plug casing. Spread prongs, then insert wire into opening in rear of core. Squeeze prongs together; spikes inside core penetrate cord to make contact with copper wires. Slide casing over plug core until core snaps into place.

How to Replace a Round-cord Plug

1 Cut off old plug using combination tool. Strip outer insulation from round cord. Strip about ¾ inch of insulation from individual wires. Remove insulating faceplate from new plug. Feed cord through rear of new plug.

2 Tie underwriter's knot in black and white wires (page 40). Use needlenose pliers to hook copper end of the black wire clockwise around the brass screw, and white wire around silver screw. On 3-prong plug, attach third wire to ground screw.

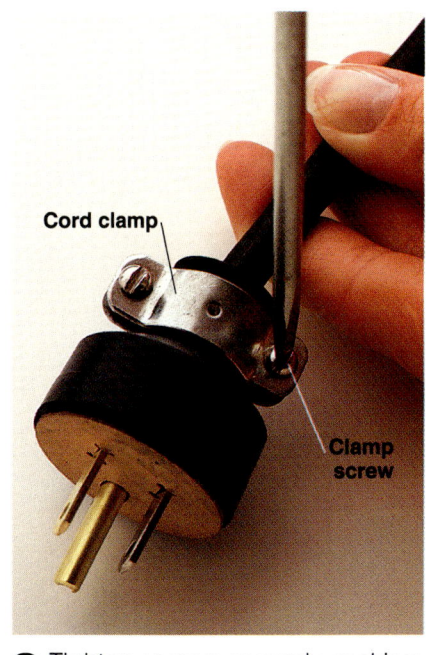

3 Tighten screws securely, making sure copper wires do not touch each other. Replace insulating faceplate. If plug has cord clamp, tighten clamp screws securely.

Replacing a Lamp Socket

Next to the cord plug, the most common source of trouble in a lamp is a worn light bulb socket. When a lamp socket assembly fails, the problem is usually with the socket-switch unit, although replacement sockets may include other parts you do not need.

Lamp failure is not always caused by a bad socket. You can avoid unnecessary repairs by checking the lamp cord, plug and light bulb before replacing the socket.

Before You Start:

Tools & Materials: replacement socket, continuity tester, screwdriver.

Tip: When replacing a lamp socket, you can improve a standard ON-OFF lamp by installing a three-way socket.

Types of Sockets

Socket-mounted switch types are usually interchangeable: choose a replacement you prefer. Clockwise from top left: twist knob, remote switch, pull chain, push lever.

How to Repair or Replace a Lamp Socket

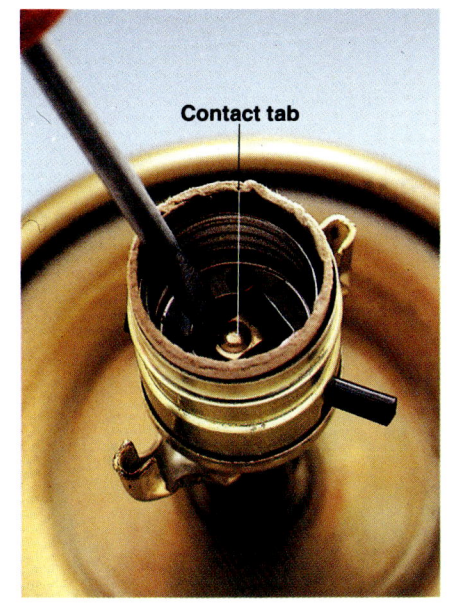

1 Unplug lamp. Remove shade, light bulb and harp (shade bracket). Scrape contact tab clean with a small screwdriver. Pry contact tab up slightly if flattened inside socket. Replace bulb, plug in lamp and test. If lamp does not work, unplug, remove bulb and continue with next step.

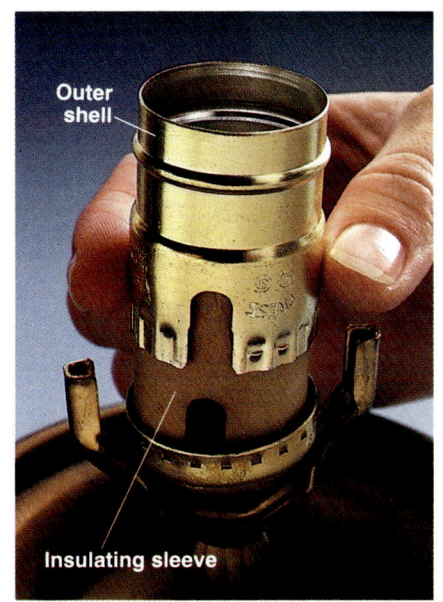

2 Squeeze outer shell of socket near PRESS marking, and lift it off. On older lamps, socket may be held by screws found at the base of the screw socket. Slip off cardboard insulating sleeve. If sleeve is damaged, replace entire socket.

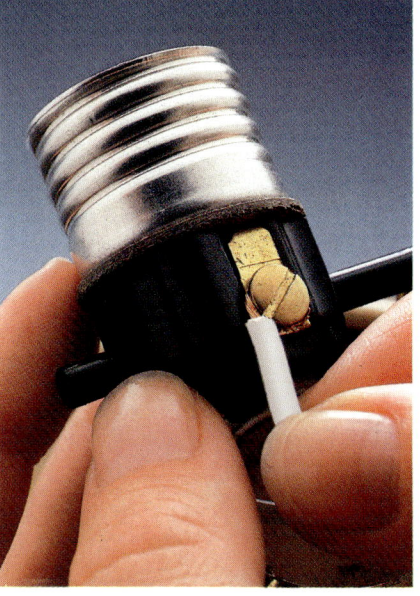

3 Check for loose wire connections on screw terminals. Refasten any loose connections, then reassemble lamp and test. If connections are not loose, remove the wires, lift out the socket and continue with the next step.

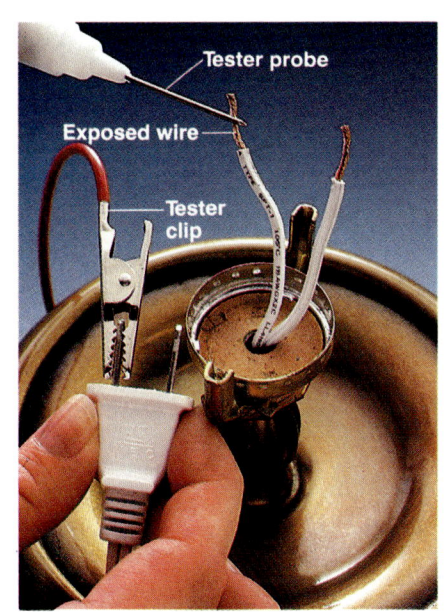

4 Test for lamp cord problems with continuity tester. Place clip of tester on one prong of plug. Touch probe to one exposed wire, then to the other wire. Repeat test with other prong of plug. If tester fails to light for either prong, then replace the cord and plug. Retest the lamp.

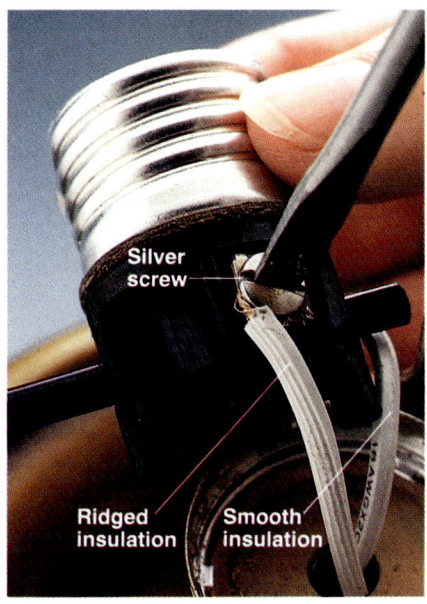

5 If cord and plug are functional, then choose a replacement socket marked with the same amp and volt ratings as the old socket. One half of flat-cord lamp wire is covered by insulation that is ridged or marked: attach this wire to the silver screw terminal. Connect other wire to brass screw.

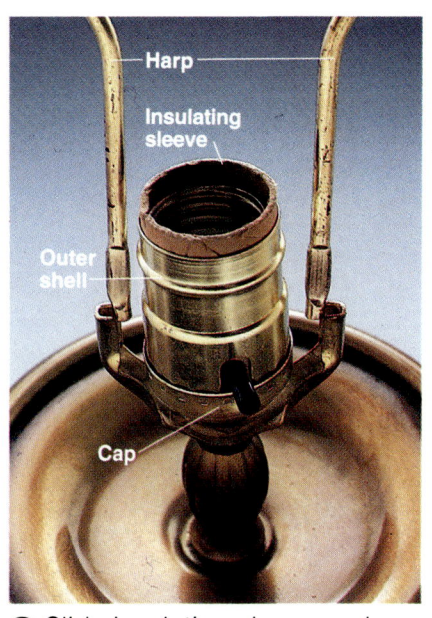

6 Slide insulating sleeve and outer shell over socket so that socket and screw terminals are fully covered and switch fits into sleeve slot. Press socket assembly down into cap until socket locks into place. Replace harp, light bulb and shade.

45

Replacing a Receptacle

Replace a receptacle when it no longer grips a plug, if it carries no power or when the inner contacts may be corroded. If a fuse or circuit breaker trips when you plug an appliance into a certain receptacle, replace the receptacle immediately.

You may want to replace a receptacle even though it still works. Older 2-slot receptacles may not accept modern appliance plugs. Install a modern safety device called a ground-fault circuit interrupter (GFCI) in outlets located near a water source or plumbing pipes.

> **Before You Start:**
>
> Tools & Materials: replacement receptacle, circuit tester, screwdriver, masking tape.

Types of Standard Electrical Receptacles

Older 2-slot receptacles should be replaced by 3-prong receptacles when they fail, but first make sure the outlet is grounded (page 39). If it is not grounded, call an electrician to update the outlet.

Grounded receptacles contain two vertical slots and one round slot. Choose a replacement receptacle with the same amp, volt and wire gauge ratings as old receptacle (page 39).

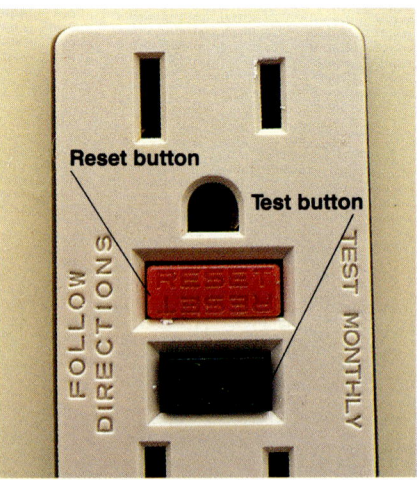

GFCI receptacle senses tiny changes in current and shuts off power before shock can occur. GFCI is installed in the same way as standard 3-prong receptacle. Test GFCI once a month: Press test button. Reset button will pop out if receptacle is operating properly.

How to Replace a Receptacle

1 Turn off power to outlet at main service panel (page 38). Remove coverplate. To test for current, carefully touch probes of circuit tester to top screw terminals on sides of receptacle. Repeat on bottom screws. If tester does not light, wires are safe to touch.

2 Loosen mounting screws, then grip mounting strap to carefully pull receptacle from box. Use small tabs of masking tape to note where each wire is attached to receptacle.

3 Release push-in connections by inserting tip of small screwdriver into release slot; or loosen screw terminals and remove the receptacle from wires.

4 Choose replacement receptacle with same ratings as old receptacle. Attach wires to receptacle (page 41) using tape markings as a guide.

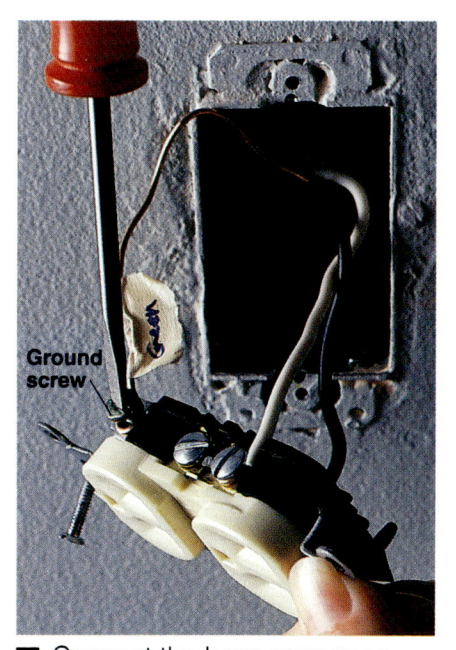

5 Connect the bare copper or green insulated wire to ground screw terminal. If box contains two ground wires, attach a green pigtail wire to the ground screw, then connect pigtail to both ground wires with a wire nut.

6 Push receptacle back into box, carefully tucking in wires. Tighten mounting screws and attach coverplate.

47

Replacing a Wall Switch

Wall switches fail when the wire connections become loose, or when mechanical parts wear out.

Begin your repair by checking the wire connections. Two or more wires are attached to the switch body by push-in or screw terminal connections. Behind the switch body, wire nuts join other similar wires, including any ground wires present.

Replace a switch that crackles or fails to operate. Switches are identified by the number of terminals on the switch body. Single-pole switches have two terminals (and occasionally a third screw for a ground connection). Three-way and 4-way switches have additional screw terminals. They are used to control a light or outlet from two or three different locations. When replacing any switch, always choose a duplicate that matches the old one.

> **Before You Start:**
>
> Tools & Materials: screwdriver, circuit tester, replacement switch, continuity tester, wire nuts.
>
> Tip: If continuity test shows that the switch is not faulty, the problem may be with the light fixture or outlet controlled by the wall switch.

How to Replace a Wall Switch

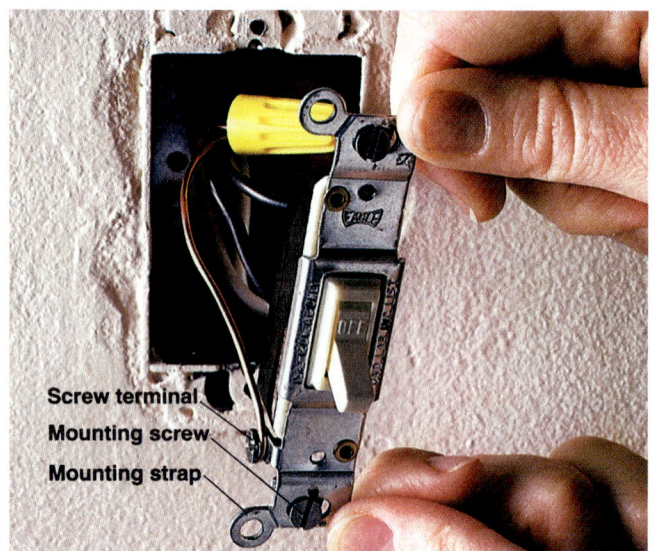

1 Turn off power to switch at main panel (page 38). Remove coverplate. Loosen mounting screws, and grip mounting strap to carefully pull switch from box. Do not touch bare wires or screw terminals.

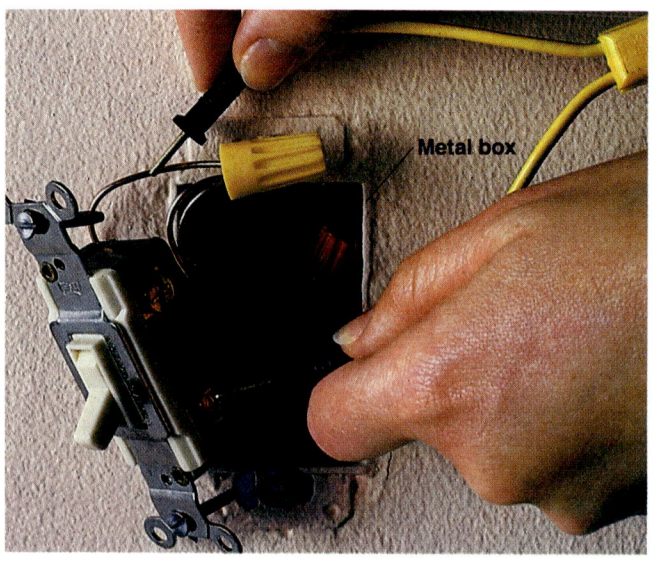

2 To test for current, touch one probe of circuit tester to screw terminal attached to a black wire. Touch other probe to the ground screw or bare copper wire, or to the metal box. Repeat test with other screw terminals. If tester does not light in any position, then wires are safe to touch.

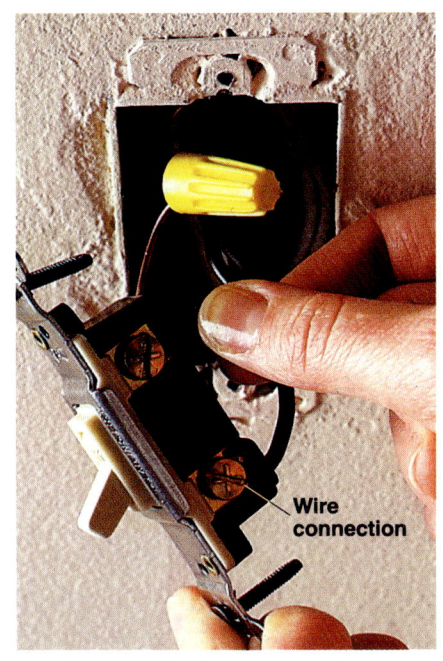

3 Check all wire connections. If loose, retighten connections, then return switch to box and test switch. If connections are not loose, then continue with the next step.

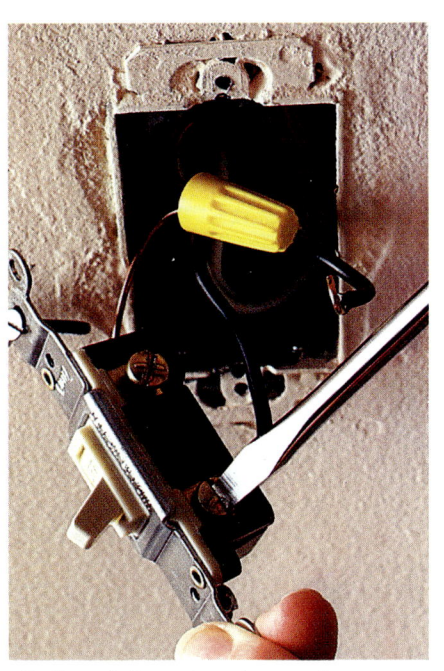

4 Carefully note where wires are attached to switch. Release wire connections, and remove switch from wires.

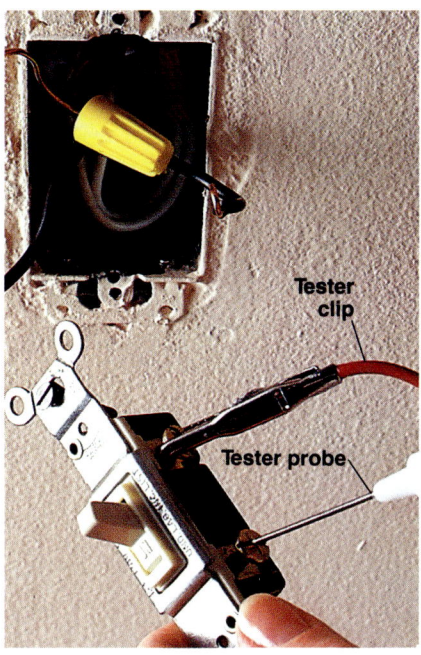

5 To test switch, attach clip of continuity tester to one screw terminal and touch probe to other screw. Flip lever. If tester does not light, replace the switch. (With 3- and 4-way switches, touch clip and probe to screw terminals of different colors.)

6 If switch is faulty, then select a replacement with same ratings as old switch. Attach wires to new switch. If new switch has green ground screw, make sure it connects to ground wire in box.

7 Push switch back into box, carefully tucking in wires. Tighten mounting screws, and attach coverplate.

Install dimmer switch using same procedure. Dimmer should have same number of wires or terminals as old switch. With 3-way dimmer, attach red dimmer wire to the black circuit wire. If dimmer has green ground wire, connect it to circuit ground wire or to metal box.

49

Replacing a Light Fixture

Replacing a wall or ceiling-mounted light fixture is one of the easiest home electrical repairs. Light fixtures usually have only two wires, connected to the circuit wires with twist-on wire nuts. Always use a steady ladder when working on ceiling fixtures, and have someone help with heavy fixtures.

Before You Start:

Tools & Materials: screwdriver, circuit tester, continuity tester, replacement fixture, wire nuts.

Tip: To avoid unnecessary repairs, check to make sure the light bulb is not burned out, is screwed in properly and that the contact tab inside the socket is not flattened. Use a continuity tester on the detached light.

How to Replace a Light Fixture

1 Turn off electricity to light fixture at main service panel (page 38). Remove globe by loosening the retaining screws. Remove mounting screws or turn fixture slightly to free it from loosened screws. Gently pull fixture away from box to expose wires.

2 Twist off wire nuts, being careful not to touch wires. To test for current, touch one probe of circuit tester to bare black wire. Touch other probe to bare white wire, then to metal box. Flip wall switch and repeat test. If tester does not light at any time, the wires are safe to touch.

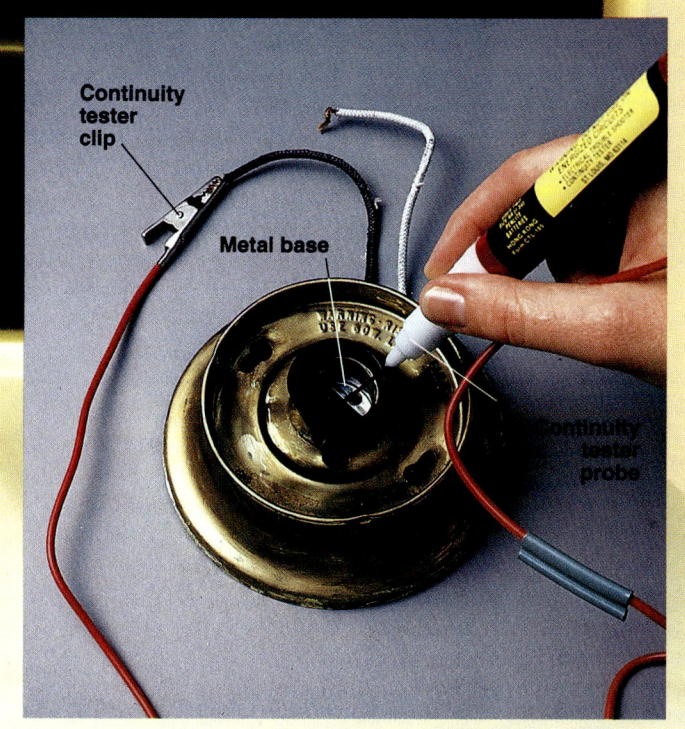

3 Untwist wires; remove fixture. Attach alligator clip of continuity tester to bare black wire, and touch probe to spring metal contact tab. Move clip to white wire and touch probe to metal base of socket. If tester fails to light in either position, then replace fixture.

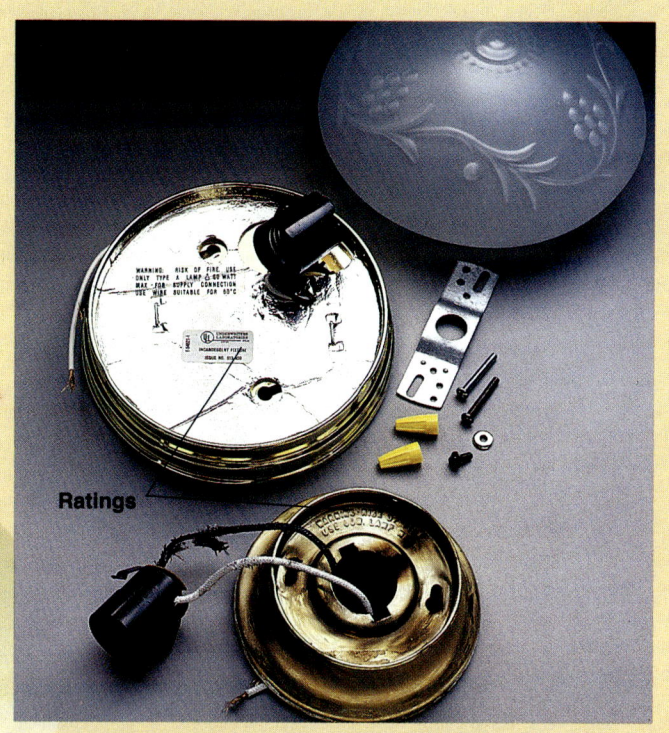

4 Select a replacement fixture that has the same ratings as old fixture. To avoid ceiling repair, choose new fixture with base as wide, or wider, than old fixture. Follow manufacturer's directions to hang new fixture.

5 Twist together copper strands of black fixture wire. Attach to black circuit wire with a wire nut. Twist together copper strands of white fixture wire, then attach to white circuit wire.

6 Make sure any insulation is in place on new fixture. Fold wires in gently, then lift light fixture flush to box. Attach and tighten mounting screws. Replace light bulb and globe.

51

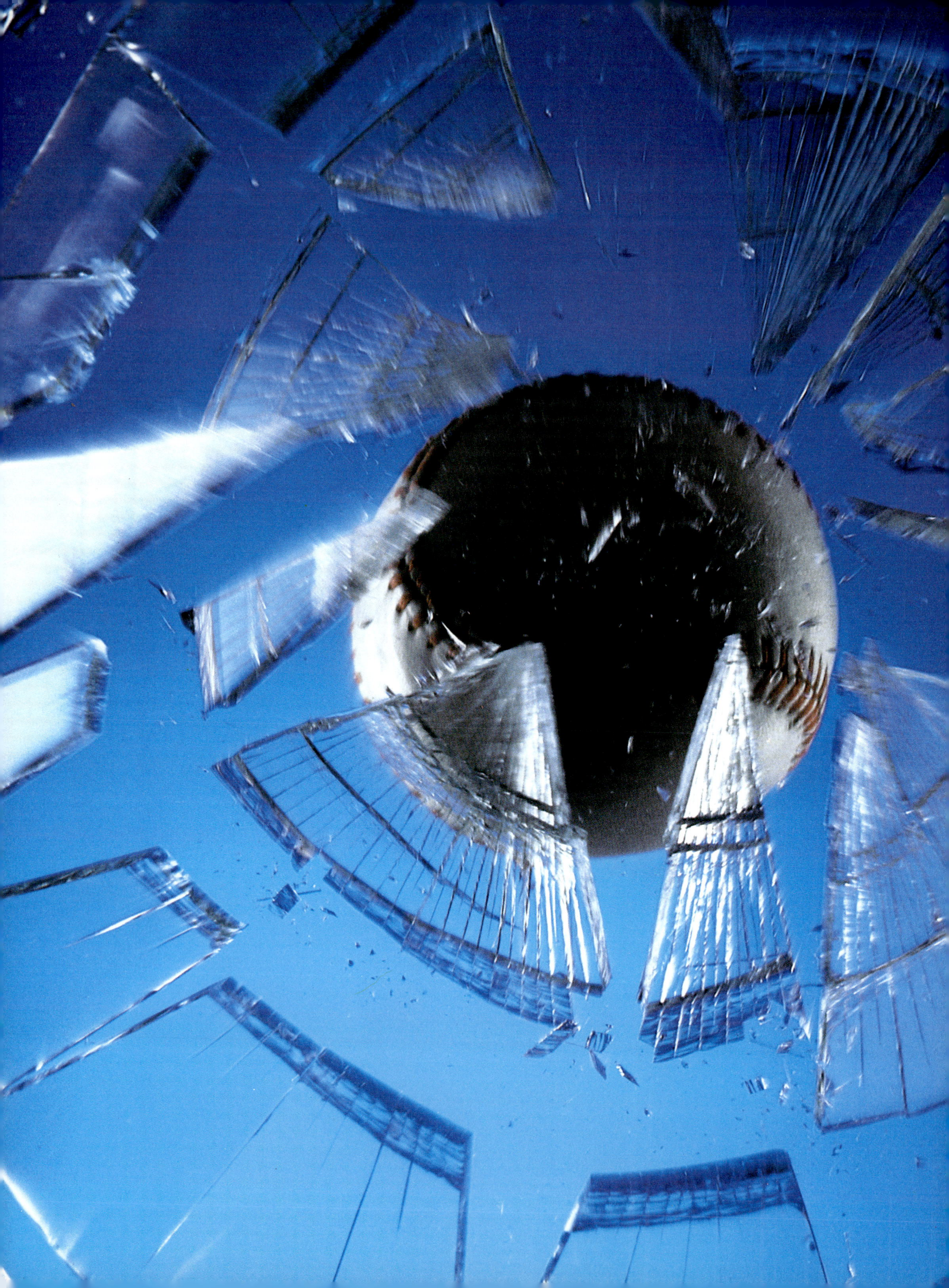

Windows & Doors

Repairing Windows & Doors

Eighty percent of all problems with window or door hardware are caused by lack of lubrication. Clean the moving parts of doors with a combination solvent/lubricant spray. Clean the tracks on double-hung and aluminum windows with an old toothbrush and a dust cloth or hand vacuum. Lubricate window tracks with a greaseless lubricant containing silicone or graphite.

Tools for Windows & Doors (Heat gun, Putty knife, Paint zipper, Glazing points, Spline, Spline roller)

Cleaners & Lubricants, from left: spray solvent/lubricant, penetrating spray, silicone spray, penetrating oils, powdered graphite (front center).

Cleaning & Lubricating Tips

Clean the tracks on sliding windows and doors with a hand vacuum and a toothbrush. Dirt buildup is common on storm window tracks.

Clean weatherstrips by spraying with cleaner and wiping away dirt. Use paint solvent to remove paint that may bind windows. Apply a small amount of lubricant to prevent sticking.

Lubricate locksets and hinges once each year by taking them apart and spraying with solvent/lubricant. Lubricate new locksets before installing them.

54

How to Clean & Lubricate Sliding Doors

1 Clean the tracks with a toothbrush and damp cloth or hand vacuum.

2 Spray a solvent/lubricant on all the rollers. Replace any bent or worn parts.

3 Check gap along bottom edge of door to make sure it is even. To adjust the gap, rotate the mounting screw to raise or lower the door edge.

How to Lubricate & Adjust Bifold Doors

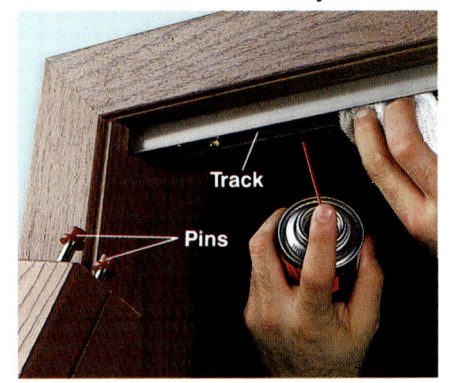

1 Open or remove the doors and wipe the tracks with a clean rag. Spray the track and rollers or pins with greaseless lubricant.

2 Check closed doors for alignment within the door frame. If gap between closed doors is not even, adjust the top pivot blocks with a screwdriver or wrench.

Adjustable pivot blocks are also found at the bottom of some door models. Adjust pivot block until gap between door and frame is even.

How to Lubricate Garage Doors

1 Clean the rollers and door tracks with a cloth, then spray with lubricant. Tighten any loose screws, bolts or nuts. **Do not** tamper with the steel springs: they are under high tension, and should be adjusted by a professional.

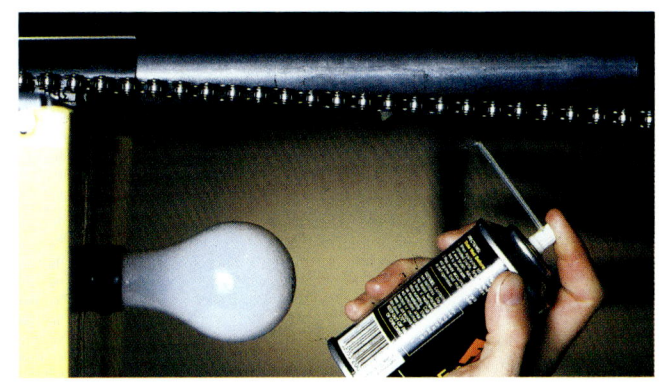

2 Clean and lubricate the drive chain and track of an automatic opener. Check manufacturer's instructions for additional maintenance directions.

Installing New Weatherstripping

Weatherstripping seals cracks between jointed or moving materials — between the window and frame, or between the door and its frame or threshold. Weatherstripping keeps dirt, insects and cold air outside your house, and keeps conditioned air (heated or cooled) inside the home. It also silences rattling doors or windows.

New weatherstripping is always a wise investment. The money you save on fuel costs in a single heating season far exceeds the purchase price of the weatherstripping.

Weatherstripping is made of a variety of materials: foam plastic, vinyl or plastic. Most types of weatherstripping are sold in kits that contain all the nails or screws needed for installation.

Before You Start:

Tools & Materials: new weatherstripping, hammer, screwdriver, tin snips, hacksaw, drill, pry bar.

Types of Weatherstripping

Spring metal provides a seal between a door and frame.

Adhesive vinyl v-stripping can be used on windows or doors.

Metal & vinyl may contain felt and attaches to window frame.

Garage door weatherstrip seals out water, dirt and insects.

Door sweeps seal gap between a door and threshold.

How to Install a Door Sweep

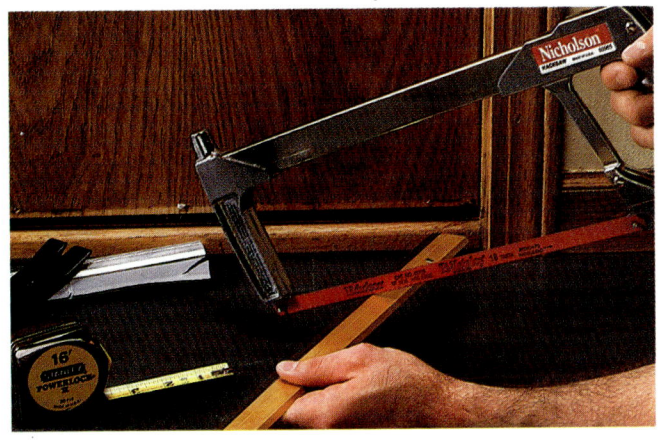

1 Measure the width of the door. Cut a new sweep with a hacksaw so that the sweep is ⅛ inch narrower than width of the door.

2 Drill pilot holes for screws, then screw sweep to inside of door so that felt or vinyl blocks gap under door. Slotted screw holes allow adjustment.

How to Install Garage Door Weatherstrip

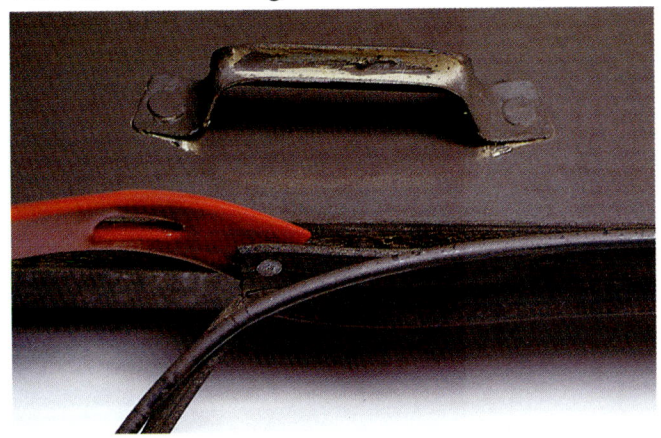

1 Remove the cracked or brittle weatherstrip by prying out old nails.

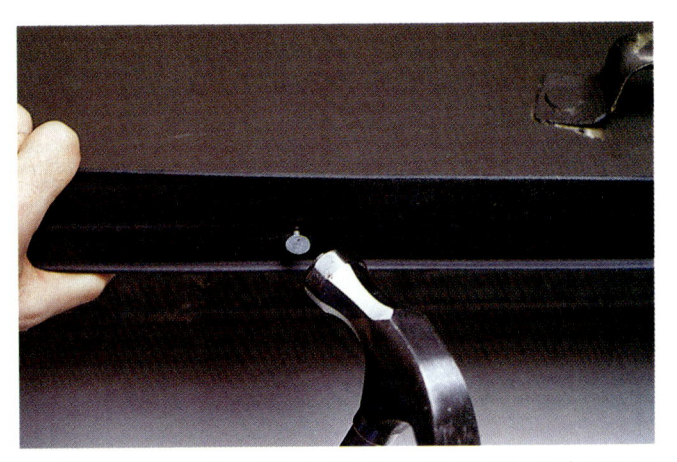

2 Cut new weatherstrip to fit door. Nail strip to bottom of door with noncorroding galvanized nails.

How to Install Spring-metal Door Stripping

1 Cut metal strips to fit the top and both sides of the door frame (jamb). Open V of strip faces outdoors.

2 Nail strips in place with slight gap between the metal and door stop. Spring metal compresses to seal air leaks when door closes.

3 Pry metal outward slightly with screwdriver to assure tight seal. Do this before each heating season, because strip gradually loses its spring.

How to Install Adhesive Vinyl V-stripping

1 Clean the window sashes and channels with a dry cloth. Remove any worn weatherstripping.

2 Cut vinyl v-strips for the window channels. Strips should measure 2 inches longer than window sash. Crease each strip into a V shape.

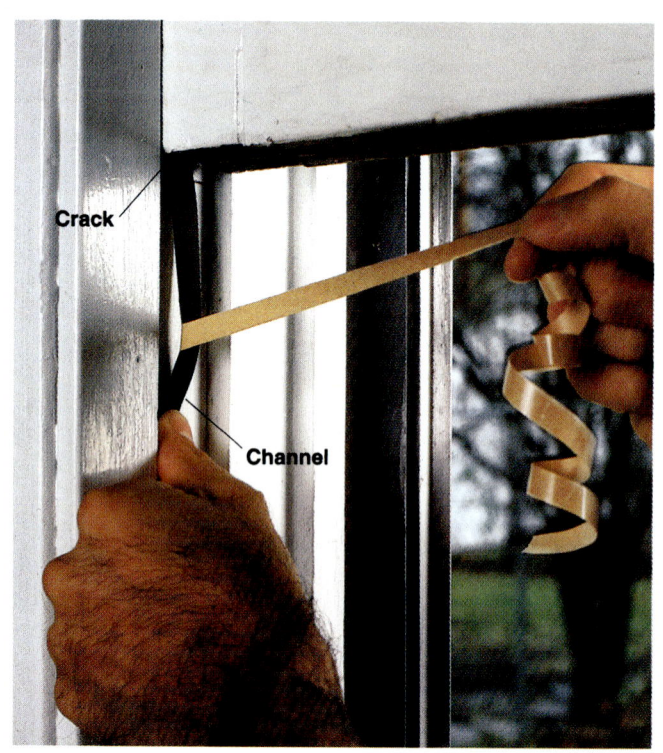

3 Open lower window fully. Tuck top end of v-strips into cracks between window and channel, with open V facing outdoors. Peel off liner, beginning at bottom, and press v-strip in place.

4 Cut strip to fit bottom sash. Peel liner and press v-strip onto bottom sash.

58

5 Cut v-strip to fit the lock rail of the top window. Crease strip, then peel liner.

6 Press v-strip into place. Open V of strip should face down. On newer double-hung windows, the bottom window can be removed to install v-strips.

How to Install Metal & Vinyl Stripping

1 Cut the strip long enough so that one piece will seal entire opening.

2 Bend strip sharply to fit corners. Press strip against window sash so that vinyl compresses slightly.

3 Nail weatherstrip around opening. At corners, nail close to corner to assure tight seal.

Repairing Loose or Sticking Windows

Windows stick because the channels or guides need cleaning and lubricating, or because they have been painted shut.

Loose windows that refuse to stay open may have broken sash cords or chains.

Newer double-hung windows are balanced by springs, and have adjustment screws to control window movement.

Before You Start:

Tools & Materials: paint zipper or utility knife, hammer, screwdriver, small pry bar, sash cord.

Tips for Freeing a Sticking Window

Cut paint film, if window is painted shut. Insert a paint zipper or utility knife into crack between window stop and sash.

Place block of scrap wood along window sash. Tap lightly with a hammer to free window.

How to Adjust Spring-loaded Windows

Adjust screw found on track insert. Turn screw until window is properly balanced.

60

How to Replace Broken Sash Cords

1 Cut any paint seal between the window frame and stops using a utility knife or paint zipper. Pry stops away from frame with small pry bar, or remove molding screws.

2 Bend stops in a slight curve from center of frame to remove them. Remove any metal weatherstripping by pulling nails holding strips in channel.

3 Slide out the lower window. Pull knotted or nailed cords from holes in side window sashes.

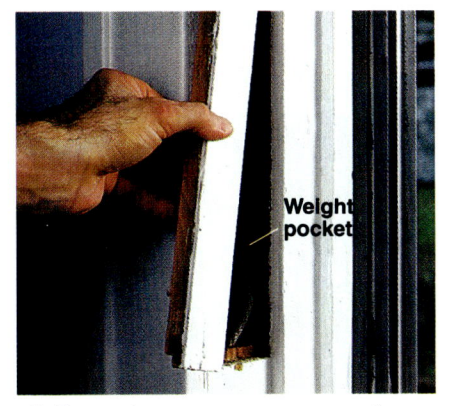

4 Pry out or unscrew cover of weight pocket found in lower end of window channel. Reach inside pocket and remove the weight. Remove old sash cord from weight.

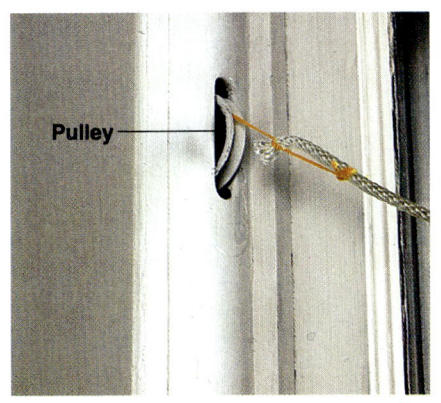

5 Tie piece of string to small nail. Tie other end of string to new sash cord. Run nail over the pulley wheel and let it drop into weight pocket. Retrieve nail and string through open pocket.

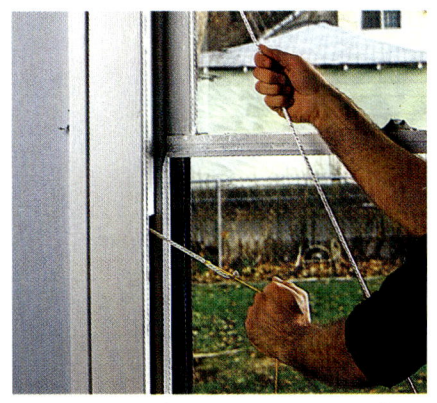

6 Pull on string to run new sash cord over pulley wheel and through weight pocket. Make sure new cord runs smoothly over pulley wheel.

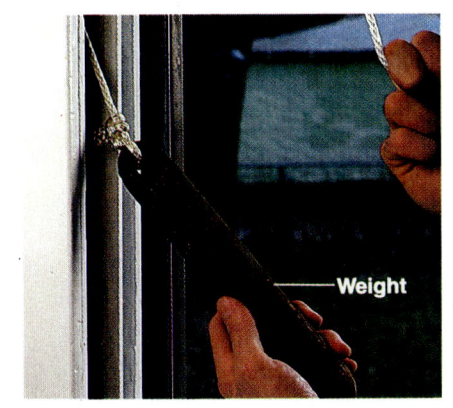

7 Attach end of new sash cord to the weight using a tight double knot. Return the weight to the open pocket and pull on sash cord to raise weight up against pulley.

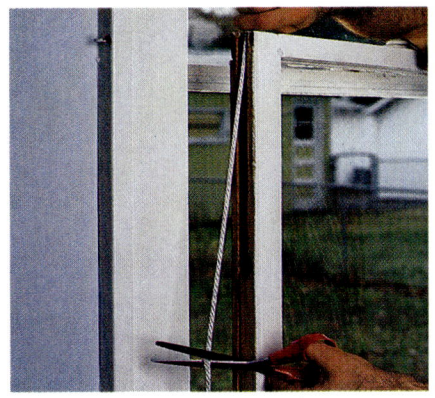

8 Rest bottom window on sill. Hold sash cord firmly against side of window, and cut enough cord to measure 3 inches past hole in side window sash.

9 Knot sash cord and wedge knot into hole in window sash. Replace the pocket cover. Slide window and weatherstripping back into frame. Nail weatherstripping and replace stops.

61

Replacing Glass

To replace broken glass, first remove the glazing putty and glazing points, then carefully remove the glass. Take the exact measurements of the opening to the hardware store. Remember that the replacement glass should measure ¼ inch less in each direction than the actual opening. This provides a ⅛-inch expansion space on each edge of the installed glass.

Seal the bare wood before installing new glass to prevent wood rot and to assure the glazing does not dry out prematurely. New types of glazing are applied by a caulk gun and are easier to work with than old-style glazing putty.

Before You Start:

Tools & Materials: heat gun, gloves, eye protection, putty knife, sandpaper, wood sealer, sash brush, replacement glass, glazing points, tube-style glazing compound, caulk gun.

Tip: To avoid injury, wear gloves and eye protection when removing broken glass from sashes, or handling new glass.

How to Install New Glass

1 Remove spring-loaded double-hung windows by pushing against flexible vinyl channels to release channel pins. Older double-hung windows can be repaired while window remains in frame.

2 With traditional glazing, soften old putty with heat gun or torch, being careful not to scorch wood. Scrape away soft putty with a putty knife. On newer windows, pry out the vinyl glazing strips.

3 Remove the broken glass and metal glazing points from the frame, then sand the L-shaped grooves to clean away old paint and putty. Coat bare wood with sealer and let dry.

4 Apply a thin layer of glazing compound in the primed grooves. Press glass lightly to bed it. Press in new glazing points every 10 inches with tip of putty knife.

5 Apply glazing compound. Move the tube tip along the edge of the glass while steadily squeezing the trigger. Smooth the glazing with wet finger or cloth.

6 Latex glazing can be painted the same day. Overlap the paint onto the glass by 1/16 inch to improve its weather seal.

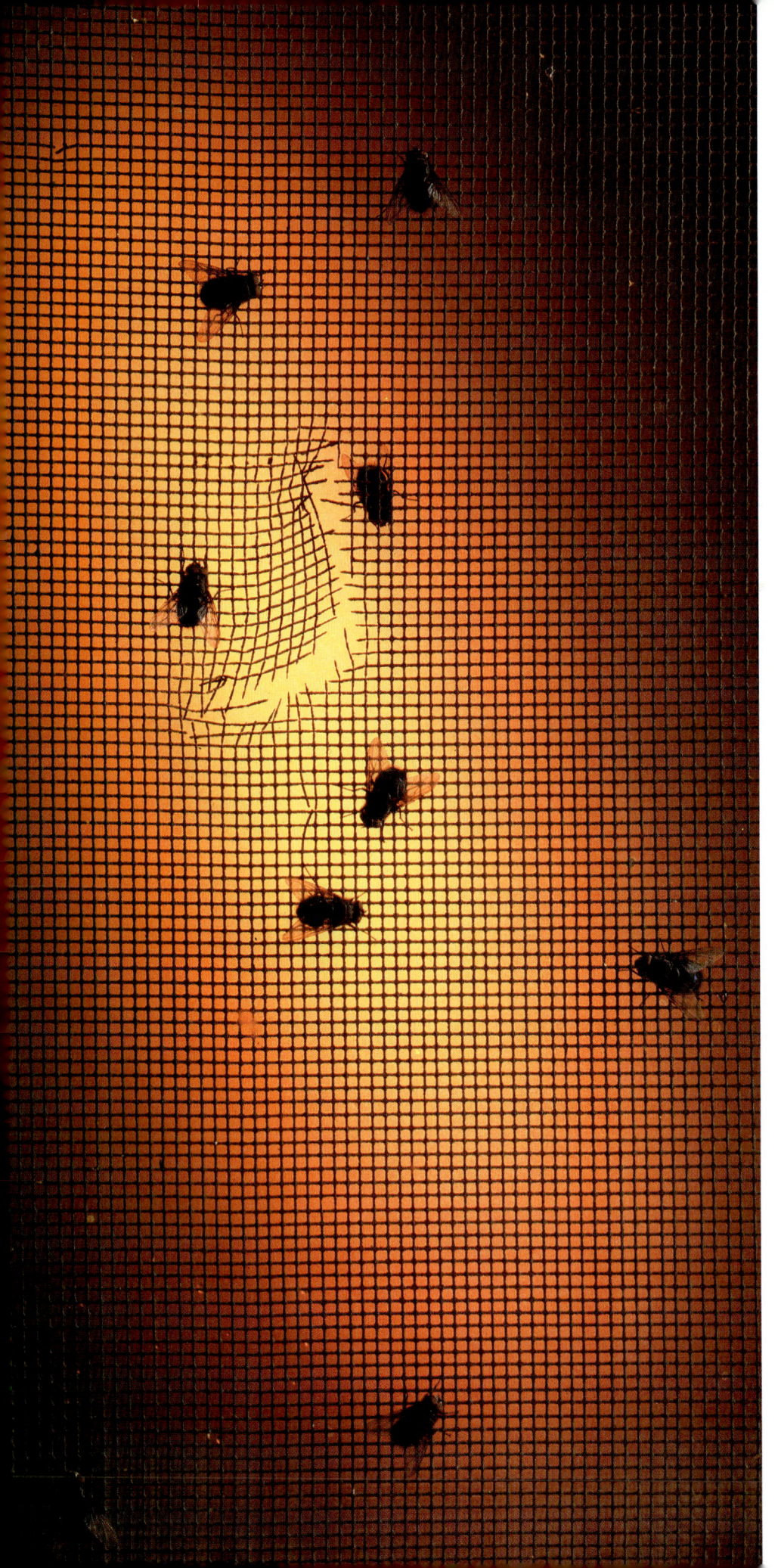

Replacing Screens

Replace the old metal screening with new fiberglass sunscreen. This blocks sunlight to keep the house cooler and prevent fabric fading. Modern screens are corrosion-resistant and maintenance-free.

> **Before You Start:**
>
> **Tools & Materials for Wooden Frames:** small chisel or screwdriver, utility knife, screen fabric, stapler or thumbtacks, wire brads, hammer.
>
> **Tools & Materials for Aluminum Frames:** screwdriver, screen fabric, vinyl spline, spline roller, utility knife.

Screen repair tip: For easy handling, cut screen fabric larger than opening, then trim after screen molding or spline is reinstalled.

How to Replace a Screen in a Wooden Frame

1 Pry up screen molding with a small chisel or screwdriver. If molding is sealed with paint, use a utility knife to cut the paint film and free the molding.

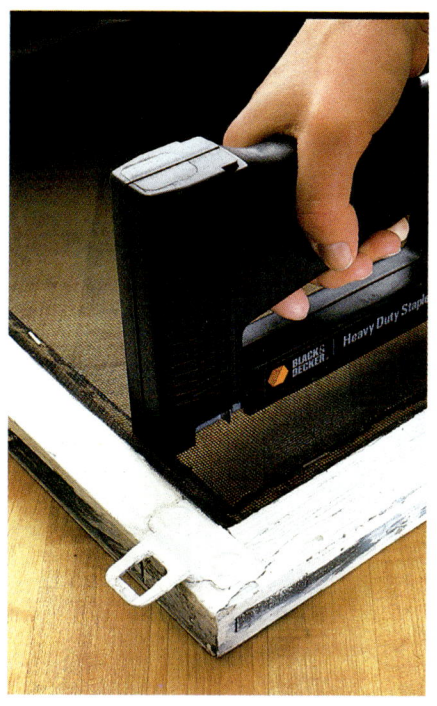

2 Stretch the new screen fabric tightly across the frame and hold it in place with staples or thumbtacks.

3 Nail the screen molding back in place with wire brads. Cut away excess screen fabric with a utility knife (page opposite).

How to Replace a Screen in an Aluminum Frame

1 Pry vinyl spline from grooves around edge of frame with a screwdriver. Retain the old spline, if it is still flexible, or replace with new spline.

2 Stretch the new screen fabric tightly over the frame so that it overlaps the retaining grooves.

3 Use a spline roller to press spline and screen into grooves. Cut away excess screen fabric with a utility knife (page opposite).

65

Repairing a Lockset

How to Clean & Lubricate Locksets

Most lockset problems are solved by cleaning away dirt buildup, then lubricating the inner parts with an all-purpose solvent/lubricant.

When a door will not latch even though the lockset is working smoothly, look for problems with the wood, hinges, strike plate or frame (pages 68-71).

Before You Start:

Tools & Materials: screwdriver, spray solvent/lubricant.

Tip: If the handle on an older passage lock falls off the spindle, rotate handle to different position on spindle, and retighten setscrew.

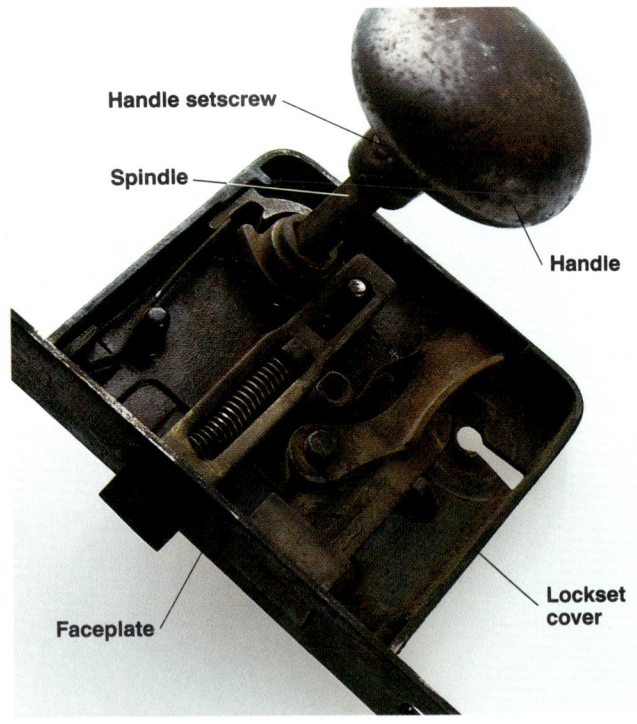

Older passage lockset. Loosen handle setscrew and remove handles and attached spindle. Loosen faceplate screws and pry lockset from door. Remove lockset cover or faceplate. Spray solvent/lubricant on all parts. Wipe away the excess lubricant and reassemble lockset.

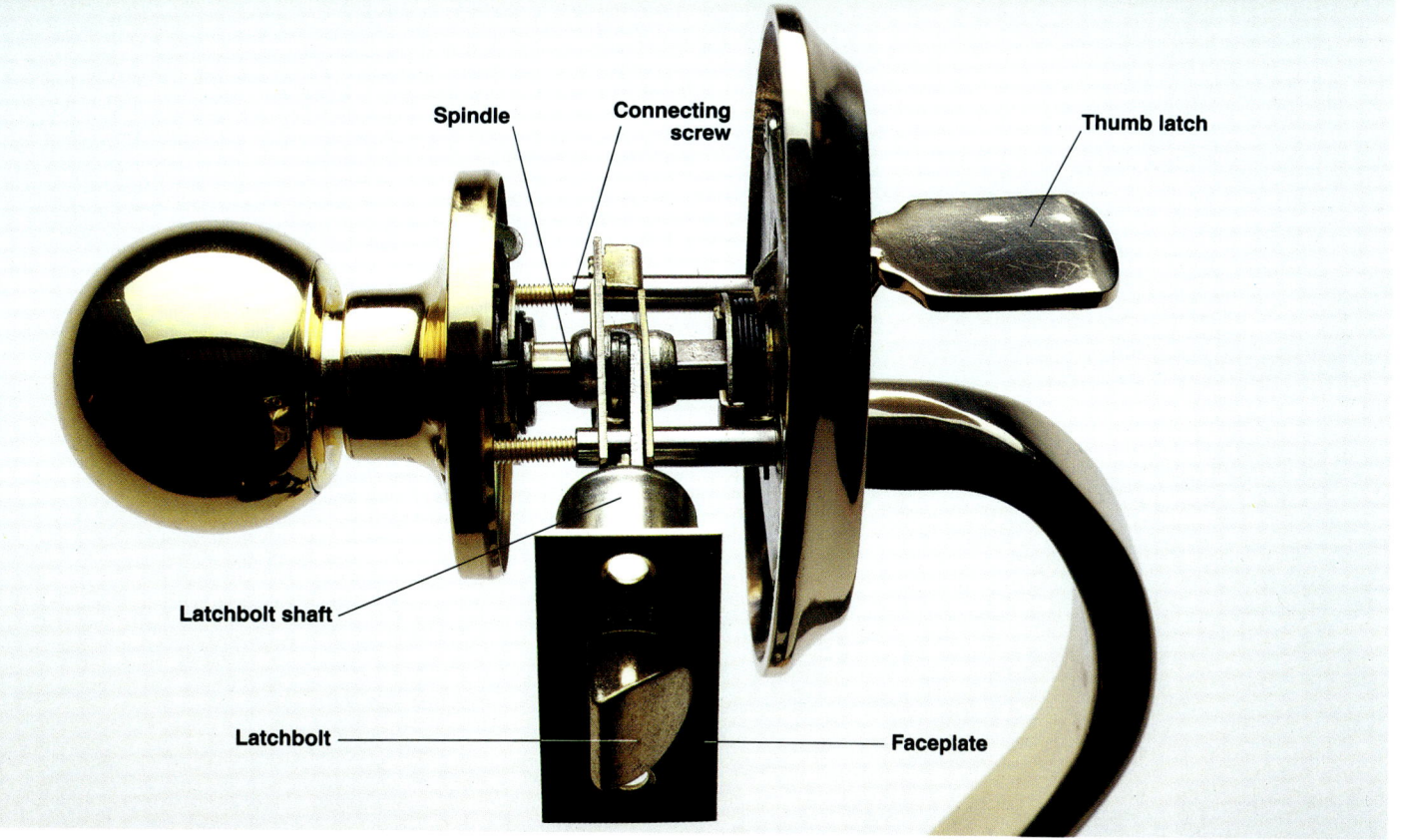

Locksets operate by extending a **latchbolt** through a **faceplate** into a strike plate set into the doorframe. The latchbolt is moved back and forth by a **spindle** or connecting rod operated by a **thumb latch, handle,** or a keyed cylinder.

If a doorknob or key binds when turned, the problem usually lies in the **spindle and latchbolt mechanism.** Cleaning and lubricating the moving parts will correct most problems.

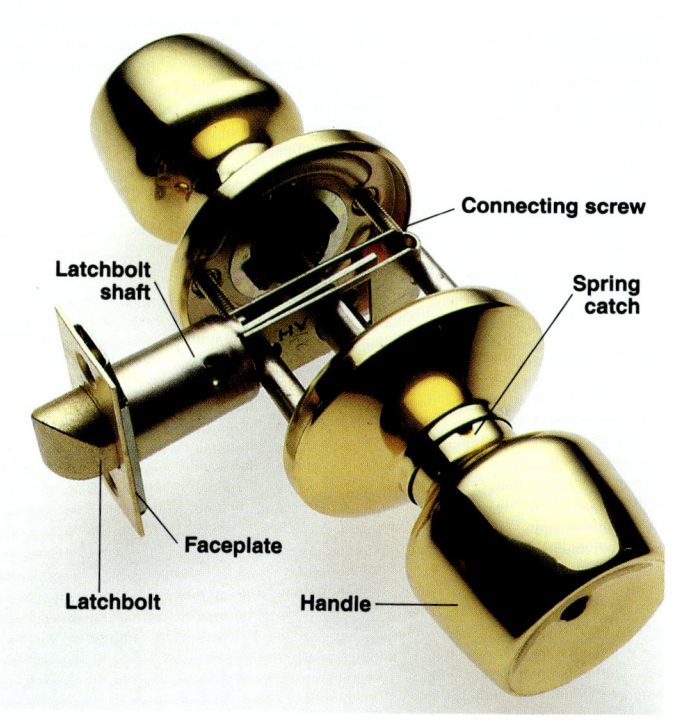

Modern passage lockset. Remove the handles (held by connecting screws or spring catch). Loosen the retaining screws to remove the faceplate and latchbolt shaft. Spray solvent/lubricant on all parts. Wipe away the excess lubricant and reassemble lockset.

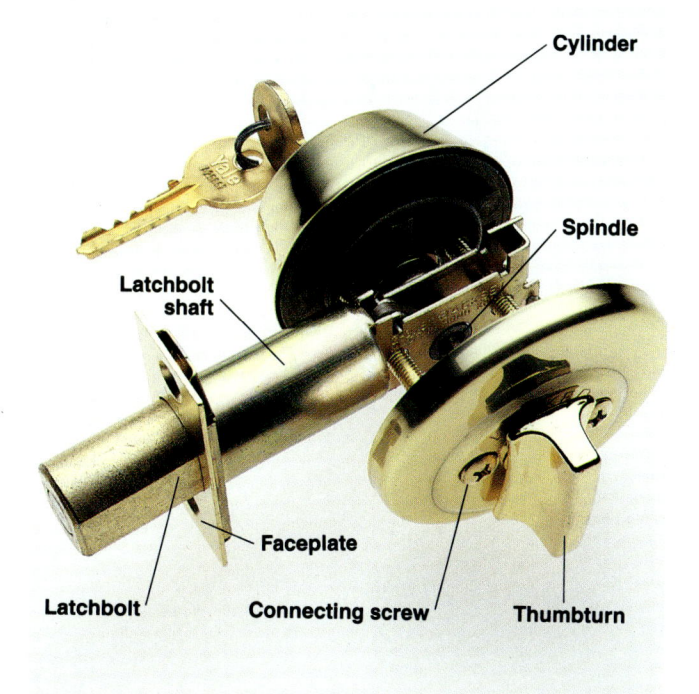

Security locks. Loosen connecting screws to remove inside and outside cylinders. Loosen retaining screws to remove faceplate and latchbolt shaft. Spray solvent/lubricant on all parts. Wipe away the excess lubricant and reassemble lockset.

Door Latch Repairs

Latching problems occur when the **latchbolt** binds within the **faceplate**, or when the latchbolt does not slide smoothly into the strike plate opening.

First, make sure the lockset is clean and lubricated (page 67). If latching problems continue, align the latchbolt and strike plate.

> **Before You Start:**
>
> Tools & Materials: metal file, cardboard shims, weights, wood sealer.
>
> Tip: If a latchbolt and strike plate are badly out of alignment, check for problems with the hinges (pages 70-71).

Sticking latchbolt is caused by dirt and lack of lubrication. Clean and lubricate lockset (pages 67-68). Make sure connecting screws on lockset are not too tight. An overly tightened screw will cause latchbolt to bind.

Common Causes of Door Latch Problems

Misalignment with strike plate prevents latchbolt from extending into strike plate opening. First, check for loose hinges (page 71). To align strike plate and latchbolt, see opposite page.

Warped door caused by humidity or water penetration can cause latching problems. Check for warping with a straightedge. To straighten a warped door, see opposite page.

How to Align Latchbolt & Strike Plate

1 Fix any loose hinges (page 71) and test door. Fix minor alignment problems by filing the strike plate until the latchbolt fits.

2 Check the door for square fit. If the door is badly tilted, then remove the door (page 70) and shim the top or bottom hinge (right).

3 Raise position of latchbolt by inserting thin cardboard shim behind bottom hinge. To lower latchbolt, shim behind top hinge.

How to Straighten a Warped Door

1 Remove door (page 70). Support both ends of warped door on sawhorses. Place heavy weights on bowed center. Leave door weighted for several days until the bow is straightened. Check door with straightedge (page opposite).

2 Apply clear sealer to the ends and edges of door to prevent moisture from entering wood in the future. Rehang the door.

Hinge pin

Freeing a Sticking Door

Doors stick when the hinges sag, or when the wood of the door or door frame swells or shifts.

Make sure the door hinge screws are tight. If a door continues to stick after you tighten the hinges, wait for dry weather to sand or plane the door. If the sticking problem occurs only during unusually wet weather, wait for a dry period, then seal the door edges. This should solve occasional sticking problems.

> **Before You Start:**
>
> Tools & Materials: screwdriver, hammer, spray solvent/lubricant, wooden golf tees or dowels, carpenter's glue, sandpaper, wood sealer.
>
> Tip: Lubricate the hinge pins to eliminate squeaking in doors.
>
> Tip: To tighten hinge screws without removing the door, block up the bottom of door with wood shims.

How to Remove a Door

1 Drive the lower hinge pin out with a screwdriver and hammer. Have a helper hold door in place. Drive out the upper hinge pin.

2 Remove the door and set it aside. Before replacing the door, clean and lubricate all the hinge pins.

70

How to Tighten Loose Hinges

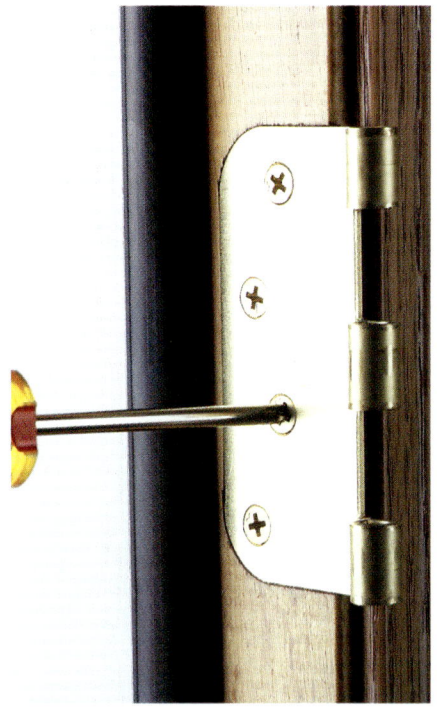

1 Remove door from hinges (page opposite). Tighten any loose screws. If wood behind hinge will not hold screws, remove hinges.

2 Coat wooden golf tees or dowels with glue and drive them into worn screw holes. Let glue dry. Cut off excess wood.

3 Drill pilot holes in new wood. Rehang hinge with new wood as base for screws.

How to Fix a Sticking Door

1 Tighten any loose hinges (above). If sticking problem continues, use light pencil lines to mark areas where the door sticks.

2 During dry weather, remove door (page opposite). Sand or plane marked areas until door fits. Seal ends and edges with clear wood sealer before rehanging door.

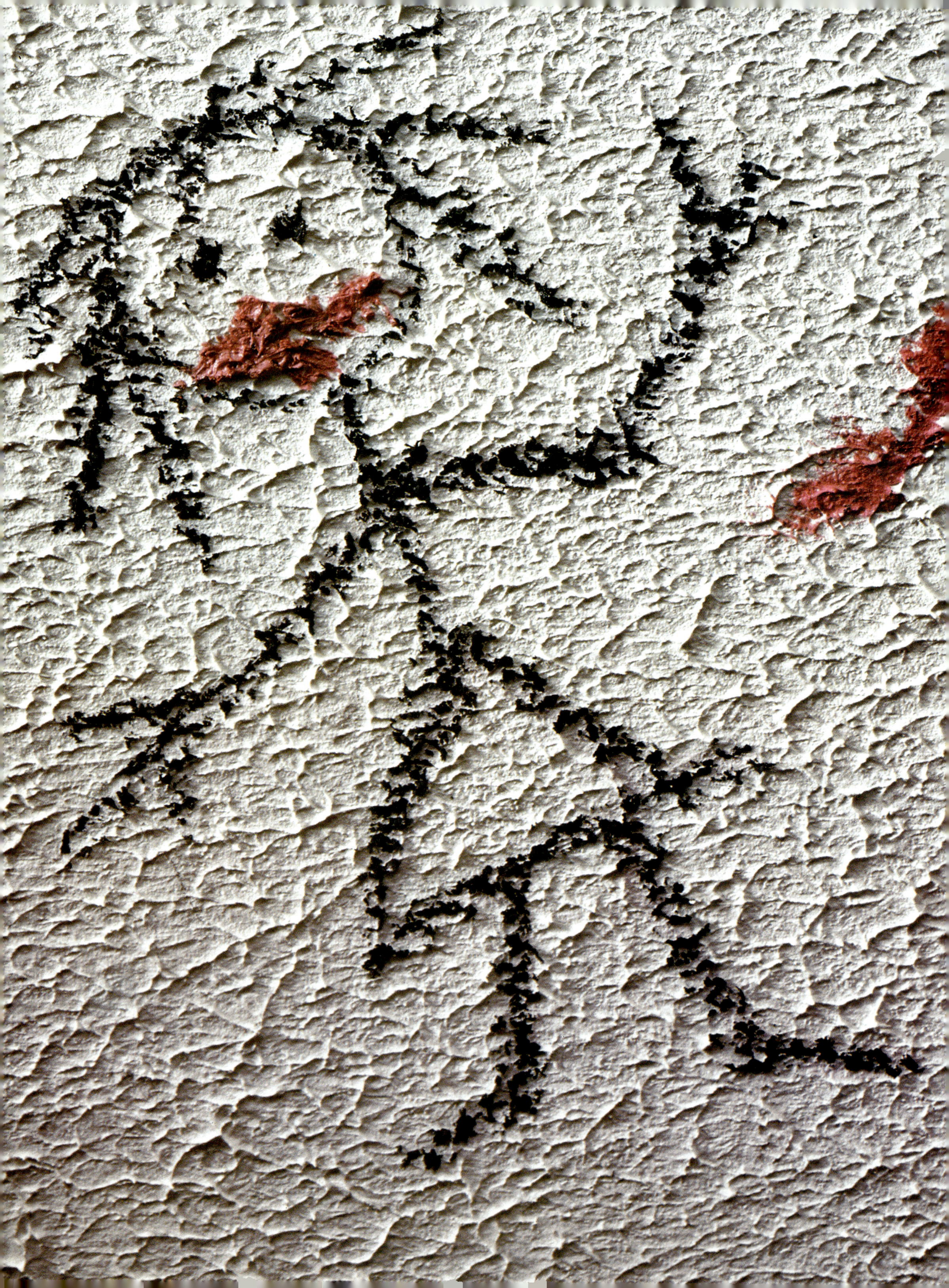

Walls & Ceilings

Walls & Ceilings

Materials for Walls & Ceilings:
- Fiberglass joint tape
- Repair patch
- Replacement tiles
- Wall hangers
- Sandpaper

The most common problems with walls and ceilings include holes, structural cracks, stains and water damage. Repairs to wallboard walls are the easiest, because damaged sections can be readily removed and replaced. But if you have plaster construction, check the overall condition of the walls and ceiling before making repairs. If the whole surface feels spongy, or if the bulges or cracks are extensive, the plaster should be covered or replaced by a professional.

For most wall and ceiling repairs, choose a pre-mixed patching plaster or taping compound that combines easy application and no-mess cleanup.

Tips for Walls & Ceilings

Latex paint spatters can be removed from most surfaces with a solvent cleaner. Test on an inconspicuous area before using it on stains.

Seal stains which bleed through paint, like lipstick, ink, oil and rust. Spray or brush clear shellac over stain. Let shellac dry completely before repainting surface.

Tools for Walls & Ceilings

How to Remove Stains from Walls & Ceilings

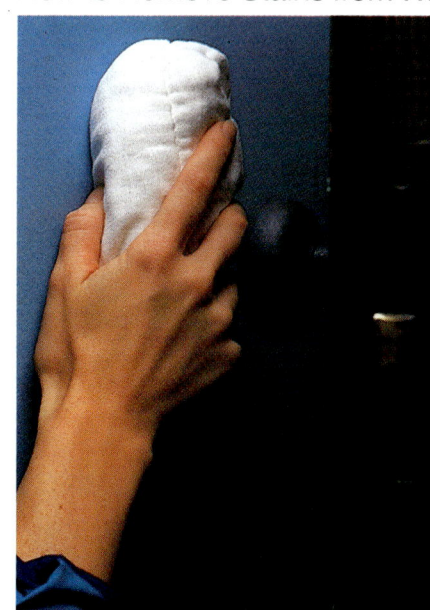

1 Test stain and graffiti removers on an inconspicuous area. Some products may alter paint or wallcovering dyes.

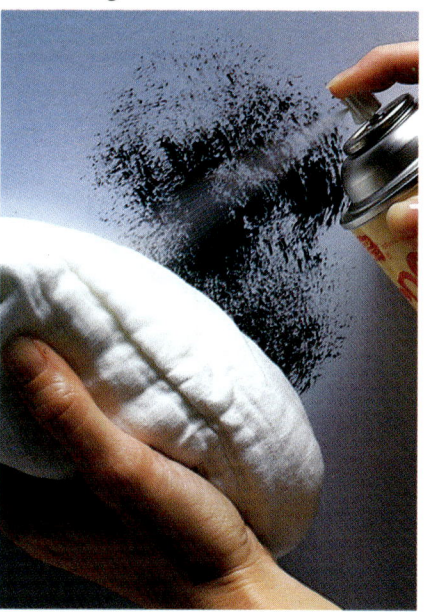

2 Spray stain remover directly on clean cloth. Dab stain area with stain remover.

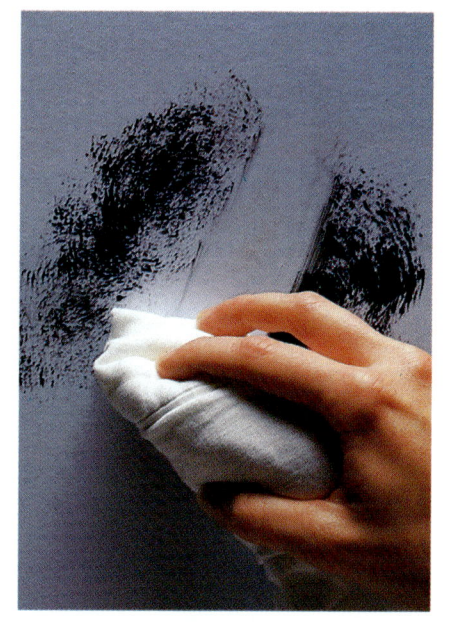

3 Wipe or blot the stain area with a clean, dry cloth. With stubborn stains, rub gently with a fiber scrub brush or pad.

75

Fastening Objects to Walls or Ceilings

Light and medium wall loads can be supported by plaster or wallboard, but heavy loads, such as bookshelves, should be anchored to studs or joists.

Studs are placed at uniform intervals of 16 or 24 inches on center: after finding one stud, measure equal distances to find the others.

When hanging some objects, such as drapery rods, there may not be a stud where you need one. To hang objects between studs, select a wall fastener designed for your type of walls and rated for the intended weight load. Fastener packages list acceptable weight loads.

Before You Start:

Tools & Materials: magnetic or electronic stud finder, wall fasteners, drill and bits, hammer, screwdriver.

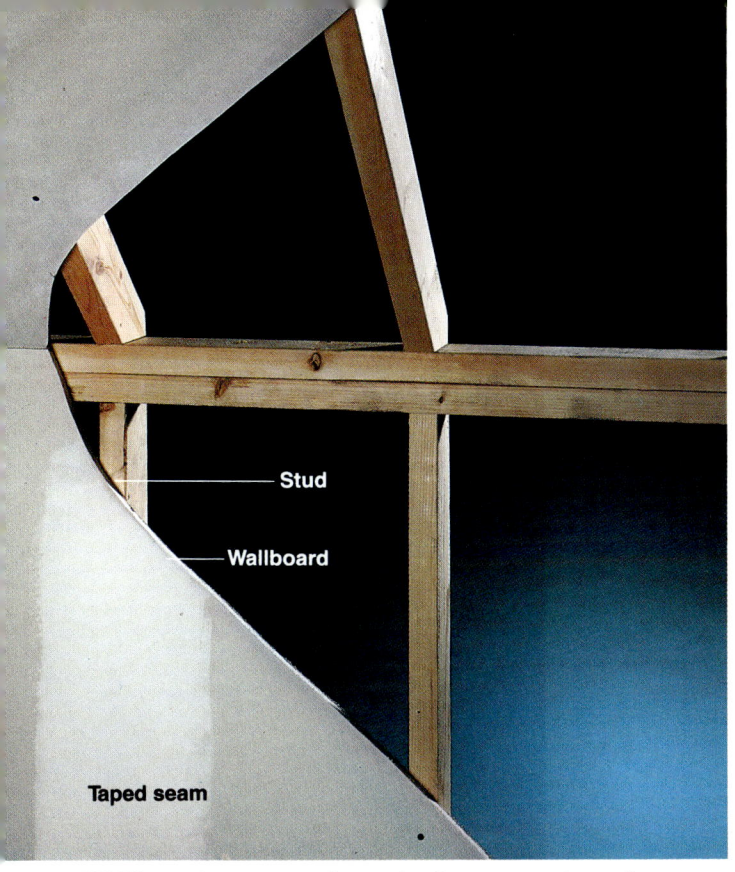

Wallboard construction, also known as drywall, uses gypsum panels nailed or screwed directly to framing members. Wallboard thickness varies from ¼" to ⅝". The studs or joists behind a wallboard surface are usually 16" or 24" apart, measured "on center." You can use a wide variety of wall fasteners in wallboard.

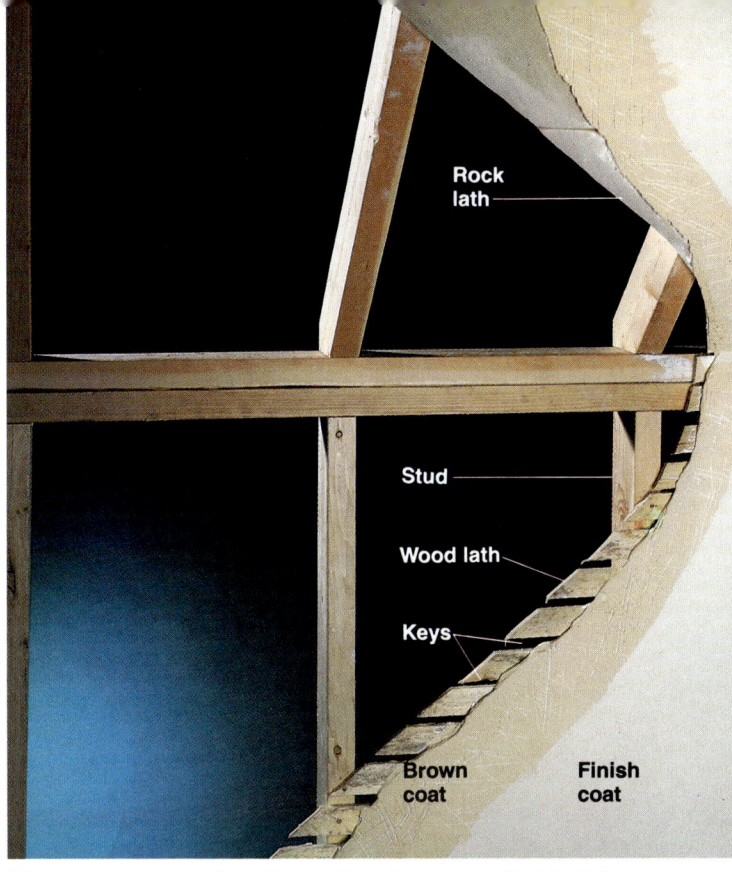

Plaster construction is applied in layers. Behind the plaster is a layer of wood, metal or rock lath which holds the plaster in place. Keys, formed when the base plaster is squeezed through the lath, hold the dried plaster to the walls and ceilings. Because plaster is a brittle surface, always drill pilot holes when hanging objects. Use screw-type fasteners whenever possible.

How to Find a Stud or Joist for Heavy Loads

Check for nails on baseboard trim, indicating stud locations. Studs are also found next to door and window frames, and along electrical outlets or light fixtures, and furnace ducts.

Use a lamp with shade removed. Sidelighting the wall with other lights turned off will reveal indentations caused by nail or screw heads attached to studs.

Use magnetic or electronic stud finder to locate steel nails. Work stud finder over the wall randomly until the magnet indicates a nail in a stud.

77

How to Hang Lightweight Objects Between Studs

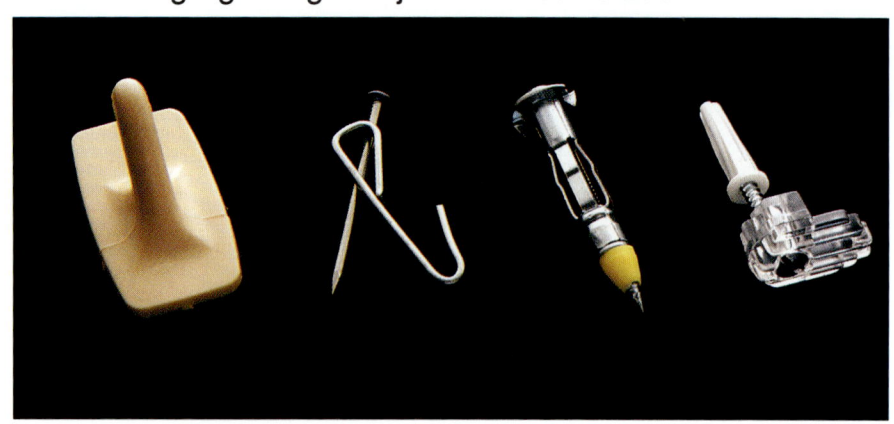

Wallhangers for light loads, from left: adhesive hook (for very light loads on untextured walls), nailed picture hanger hook, drivable molly bolt, plastic anchor with attached mirror clip.

1 Hang lightweight mirror by mounting 2 mirror clips for each corner of mirror. You will need mirror clips, plastic anchors, drill and bits.

How to Hang Mediumweight Objects Between Studs

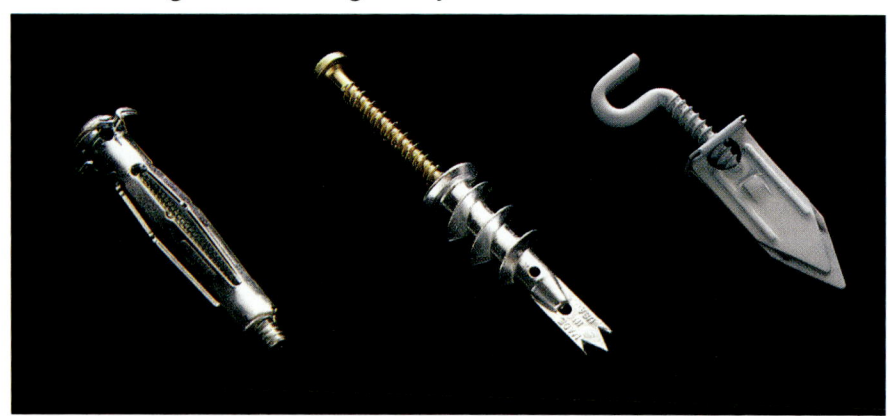

Wallhangers for medium loads, from left: molly bolt with sleeve (available in various diameters and lengths), Grip-It™ screw anchor with wallboard twist anchor, drivable wall anchor.

1 Hang mediumweight drapes using Grip-It screws when there is no wall stud. You will need drapery brackets and Grip-It screw kit.

How to Hang Heavy Objects Between Studs or Joists

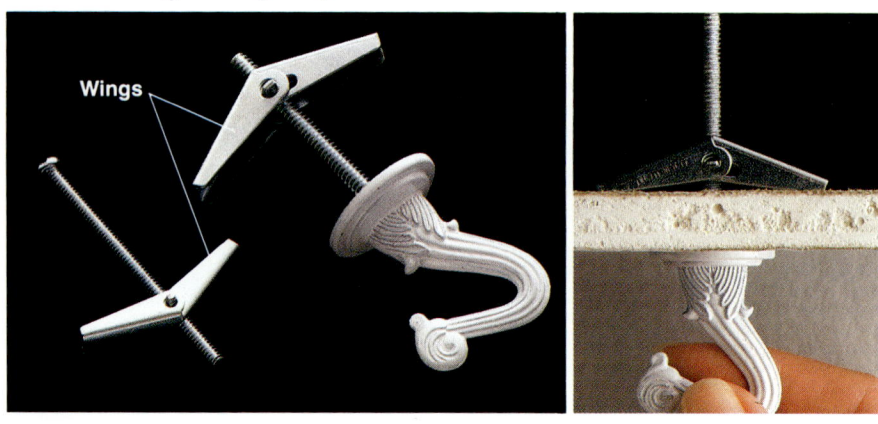

Wallhangers for heavy loads, from left: toggle bolt, headless toggle bolt with hook. Spring-loaded wings on toggle bolt collapse to fit through drilled hole, then spring open to brace against wall or ceiling as bolt is tightened.

1 Hang heavy plants using headless toggle bolt with hook. You will need drill and bit, toggle bolt with hook.

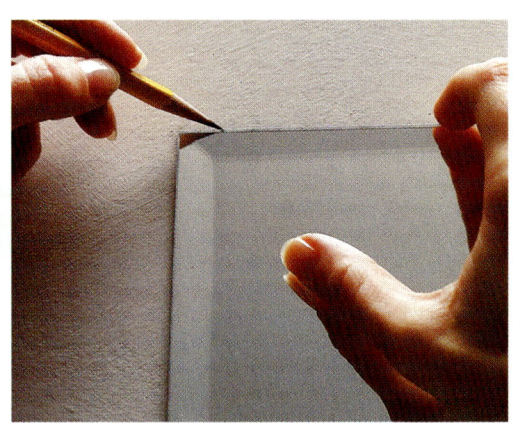

2 Hold mirror against wall, and mark corner edges of mirror with light pencil. Mark location of screw holes for mirror clips.

3 Select bit with diameter equal to plastic anchor. Drill holes with masonry bit and drive in plastic anchors.

4 Screw in bottom mirror clips. Mount mirror inside clips. Attach remaining clips.

2 Measure length of drapes to determine height of brackets. Mark location of screw holes for brackets.

3 Tap twist anchors into wallboard, then screw them in. If mounting on plaster, drill pilot holes for Grip-It screws.

4 Mount drapery brackets by driving Grip-It screw anchor into twist anchor or drilled plaster. Hang drapes.

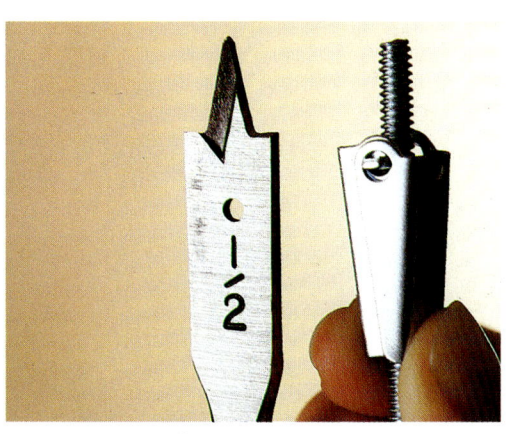

2 Select bit with diameter equal to collapsed wings of toggle bolt. Drill hole in ceiling.

3 Insert collapsed toggle bolt into hole until wings spring open. Pull bolt down slightly.

4 Attach ceiling hook to toggle bolt. Turn hook while pulling slightly, until bolt and hook are tight.

79

Repairing Wallboard

Patching holes and concealing popped nails or screws are the most common wallboard repairs. Unlike plaster, wallboard compounds will stick to painted surfaces. This means that you can patch blemishes, seams or nails directly over paint, then repaint to blend the patched area into the rest of the wall.

Before You Start:

Tools & Materials: wallboard nails or screws, screwdriver, hammer, carpenter's square, wallboard saw, scrap wallboard, hot glue gun or contact cement, fiberglass wallboard tape, premixed taping compound, wallboard knife, sandpaper or wet sander.

Tip: You can often find free wallboard scraps at construction sites.

How to Reset Popped Nails in Wallboard

Wallboard fasteners pop if they have been improperly applied, or if the framing lumber is not dry. Use screws in repairs: the threaded shanks resist popping.

1 Press the wallboard tightly against the stud or joist. Drive new screw about two inches from the popped fastener. Screw head should be indented slightly.

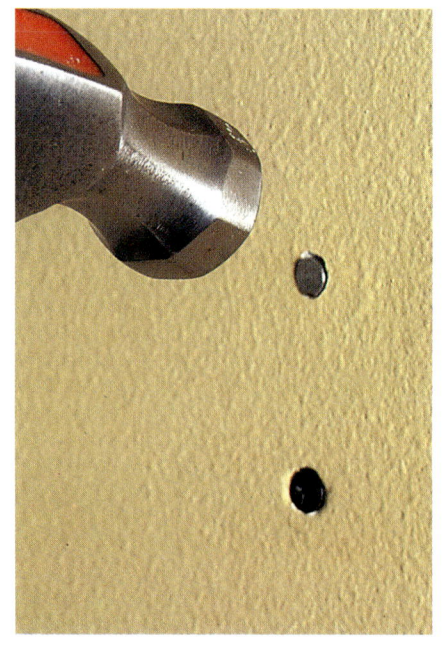

2 Hammer in the popped fastener, leaving a slight indentation. Fill dents with taping compound. Let compound dry, then repaint.

How to Patch Holes in Wallboard

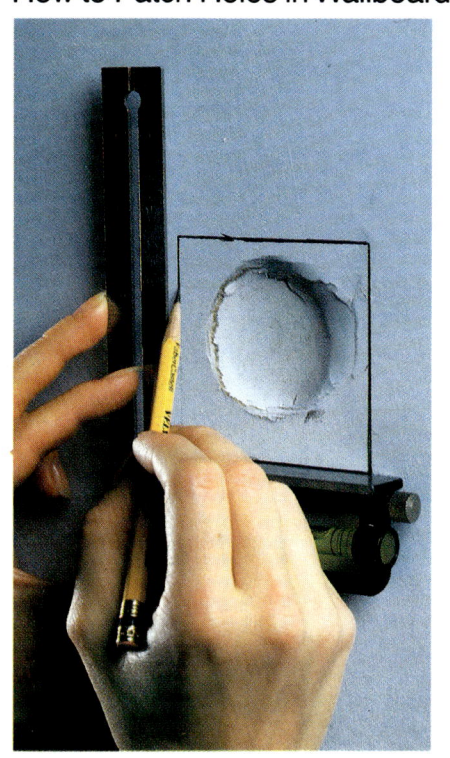

1 Outline the damaged area with a square or straightedge.

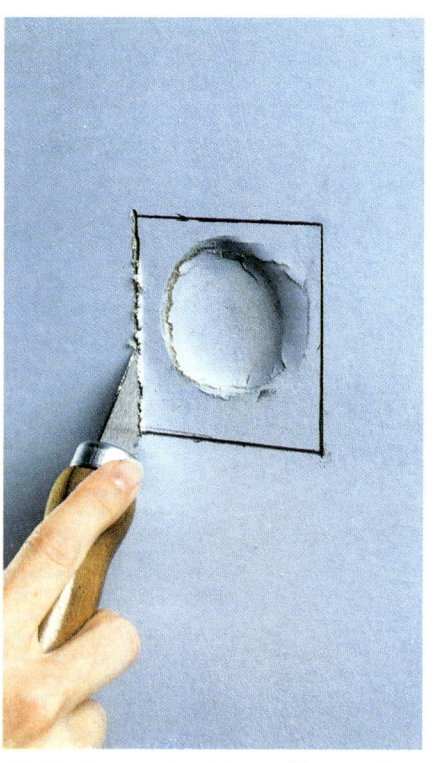

2 Cut around outline with a wallboard saw to remove damaged section.

3 Cut wallboard "backer" to hold patch. Use glue gun or contact cement to hold backer inside hole.

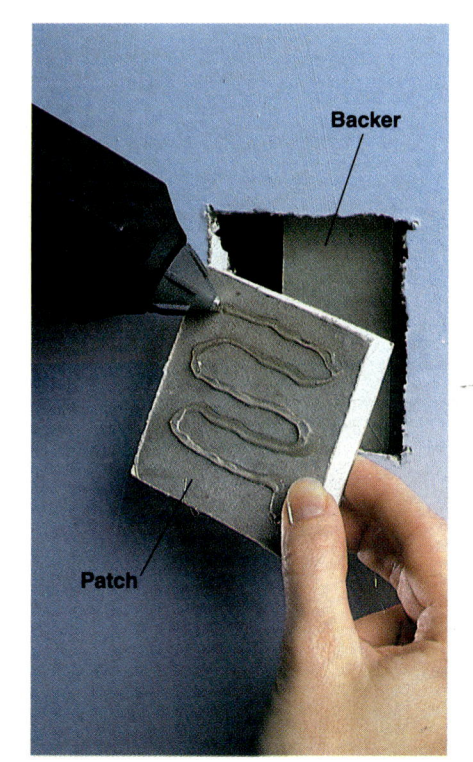

4 Cut a wallboard patch to fit opening. Patch must be same thickness as wall surface. Apply hot glue to back of patch, and press against backer until glue sets.

5 Apply fiberglass wallboard tape directly to seams. Cover tape with premixed wallboard compound using a wallboard knife.

6 Apply a second layer of compound. Let dry, then sand lightly with wet sander or sandpaper to smooth patch. Repaint wall.

Repairing Plaster

Cracks in plaster walls and ceilings are usually caused by movement in the house structure. To repair them, reinforce these cracks with a fiberglass or peel-and-stick membrane patching tape.

Holes in plaster occur because of impact damage, aging, or exposure to water. If plaster shows brown stains or powdery residue, it has been damaged by water. Check for roof damage or leaky plumbing and fix the problem before repairing the plaster.

> **Before You Start:**
>
> Tools & Materials: paint scraper, latex bonding liquid, paint brush, patching plaster, plaster trowel or wallboard knife, fiberglass wallboard tape or peel-and-stick tape, premixed wallboard compound, sandpaper, shellac sealer.
>
> Tip: Prevent bond failure and edge cracking between old and new plaster by coating patch area with latex bonding liquid before patching holes.

How to Repair Cracks in Plaster

Peel-and-stick patching tape made from thin, tough plastic membrane lets you patch and paint cracks without using plaster or taping compound. Cut patching tape slightly longer than crack. Peel off liner, then pull membrane taut and press onto crack. Hide thin tape with two coats of latex paint.

Self-adhesive fiberglass tape prevents recracking. Apply tape directly to wall and press it smooth. Use a flexible taping knife to cover fiberglass tape with one or two thin layers of premixed wallboard compound. Lightly sand patch area until smooth. Repaint.

How to Repair Holes in Plaster

1 Scrape away all loose or scaling plaster to expose firm base plaster or lath. Make sure that the damaged area does not extend beyond the scraped area.

2 Brush latex bonding liquid onto the patch area. Fully coat the edges of the old plaster. Do not wet the patch area after coating it. Mix patching plaster stiff enough for trowel application.

3 Trowel the patching plaster into hole with a wallboard knife, using a sweeping motion. Work plaster firmly into the edges of hole for a good bond. For holes ¼ inch deep or less, apply one coat of patching plaster. Let plaster set.

4 For holes deeper than ¼ inch, apply a second coat of plaster. Let plaster set, then sand lightly, if needed. Coat patch area with white shellac to seal the stain. Repaint.

Repairing Wallcoverings

Damage to wallcoverings may require that you cut and install a patch. Loosened seams and bubbles are common wallcovering problems. Although new vinyls make modern wallcoverings more durable than older "paper" coverings, occasionally they need repair. Removing stains is much easier with new vinyl surfaces.

> **Before You Start:**
>
> Tools & Materials: adhesive and applicator, roller, wallpaper dough, shellac, wallcovering remnants, utility knife, sponge.
>
> Tip: Save wallcovering remnants for future repairs, or remove patch section from an inconspicuous spot, such as a closet or behind a door.

Tips for Wallcoverings

To fix seams, lift edge of wallcovering and insert tip of glue applicator under it. Squirt adhesive onto the wall. Press edge back in place with a roller and wipe away excess adhesive with a clean, wet sponge.

Clean soiled wallcovering with wallpaper dough or a gum eraser, purchased from your decorating center.

How to Patch Wallcoverings

1 Fasten wallcovering patch material to the wall over the damaged portion with removable tape, so that the pattern aligns with the existing wallcovering.

2 Cut through both layers of wallcovering with a sharp knife to assure a perfect pattern match. Remove patch material, then apply water to damaged area of wallcovering.

3 Peel the damaged section away from the wall. Apply adhesive to the back of the patch and carefully position it in the hole so patterns match. Wipe with a clean wet sponge.

How to Flatten Bubbles

1 Cut a slit at the edge of the bubble using a utility knife. If there is a pattern in the covering, cut along a pattern line to help conceal the cut.

2 Insert tip of glue applicator under flap and apply adhesive sparingly to the wall underneath the covering.

3 Press gently to rebond the wallcovering. Use a clean wet sponge to press the flap down and wipe away excess adhesive.

Ceramic Tile Care & Repair

Ceramic tile is durable and nearly maintenance-free, but the grout between the tiles can deteriorate. Damaged grout offers the only point of water entry, and water penetration will destroy the tile base, and eventually, the entire tile job.

To avoid stains and mineral buildup on tiles, use a bath towel to wipe down the tile walls after using the bath or shower. Use an exhaust fan to remove humid air and avoid mildew and moisture damage.

Before You Start:

Tools & Materials: 3/8" variable-speed drill, carbide bit, masonry anchor, hammer, chisel, utility knife, replacement tile, tile adhesive, masking tape, grout, rubbing alcohol, awl, tub caulk.

Tip: Ceramic tile that dates before the 1960s was set in a masonry base, and repairs should be done by a professional. Remember to use protective eyewear whenever using a hammer and chisel.

How to Hang Tile Fixtures

1 Place masking tape over the spot where you want to drill. Drill hole for anchor using a carbide masonry bit and 3/8-inch variable-speed drill. Drill bit should be same size as anchor. Use low drill speed to ensure that bit does not skip on tile.

2 Tap a plastic or lead masonry anchor plug into the hole and use a screw to attach the fixture. Be careful not to chip the tile.

How to Remove & Replace Broken Tiles

1 Scrape away old grout from between the tiles with a utility knife or awl. Break tile into small pieces with a chisel and hammer for easy removal. Scrape debris and old adhesive from hole with a utility knife or sharp scraper.

2 Test-fit new tile to be sure it sits flush with the old tile. Spread adhesive on the back of the replacement tile. Place tile in the hole and twist slightly to ensure contact with wall. Use masking tape to hold tile in place overnight.

Sponge

3 Remove the masking tape. Apply premixed tile grout with a sponge or grout float. Let grout set slightly, then wipe away excess with damp cloth.

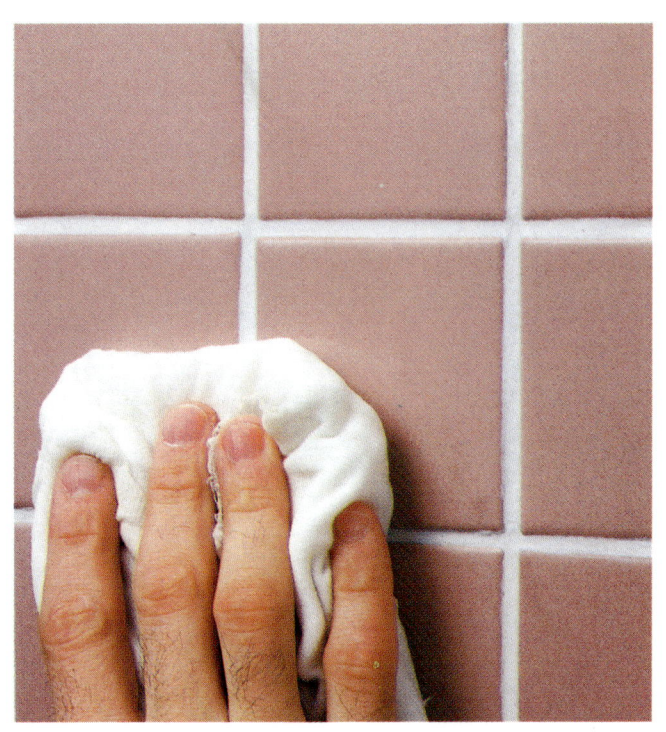

4 Let grout dry for about 1 hour. Polish the tile with a clean dry cloth to remove the powdery residue.

How to Regrout Ceramic Tile

1 Scrape out old grout with an awl or utility knife to leave a clean bed for the new grout. Remove and replace any broken tiles (page 87).

2 Clean and rinse the grout joints with a sponge. Choose premixed grout that is resistant to mildew and stains.

3 Use a foam grout float or sponge to spread grout over entire tile surface. Work grout well into joints. Let grout set slightly, until firm, then wipe away the excess with a damp cloth.

4 Let grout dry completely. Wipe away powdery residue and polish the tiles with a dry soft cloth. Apply caulk around bathtub or shower stall (page opposite). Do not use tub or shower for 24 hours.

How to Recaulk Around a Bathtub or Shower Stall

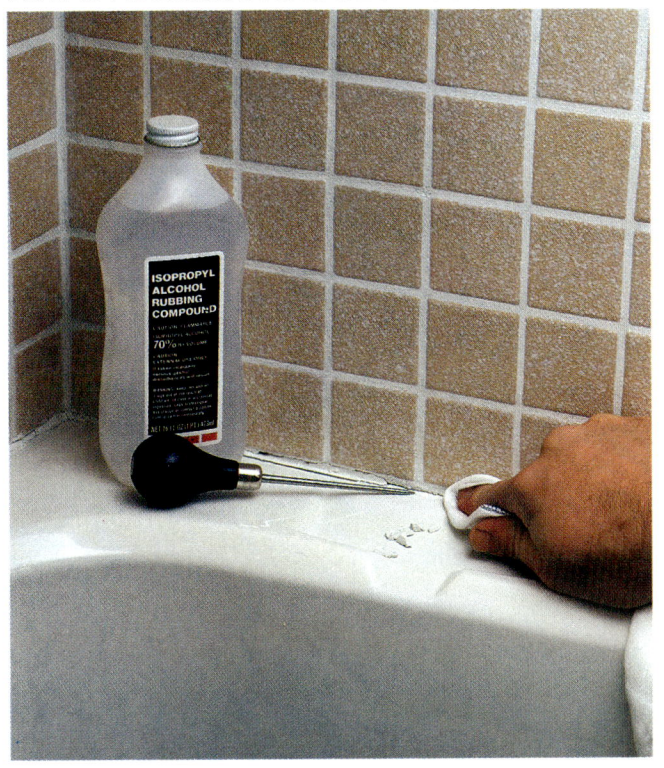

1 Scrape out old grout or caulk with an awl or can opener. Wipe away soap scum from joint with rubbing alcohol and a clean cloth.

2 Fill tub with water so it will be heavy enough to pull tub away from the tile. Fill joint with a silicone or latex caulk that will not become brittle.

3 Wet your fingertip with cold water so the caulk will not stick to your finger, and smooth the caulk into a cove shape. Let caulk harden and trim any excess away with a utility knife.

Peel-and-stick tub & tile caulks are pre-formed, reducing the work of cleaning the joint and cleaning up the new caulk. Peel the backing off and press the new caulk into place.

Floors

Floor Repairs

The most common floor repairs include removing burns or stains from carpet or hardwood, replacing or repairing damaged vinyl, restoring damaged or stained hardwood, and silencing floors and stairs that squeak.

If you saved the leftovers from a floorcovering installation, you already have the materials needed to repair small areas of damaged vinyl or carpeting. If you do not have remnants, take patch material from an inconspicuous area — a carpeted closet, or the tiled area behind a kitchen appliance.

Rental stores have floor tools such as power stretchers, glue irons for refastening loose carpet seams and carpet edge trimmers. Describe the problem, and ask the rental clerk to suggest the right tools for your project.

Tools and Materials for Floor Repair

Tips for Carpet Care

Prevent damage and excessive wear on your floors by placing a door mat at each entry. The mat prevents tracking grit onto floors, reducing wear and cleaning.

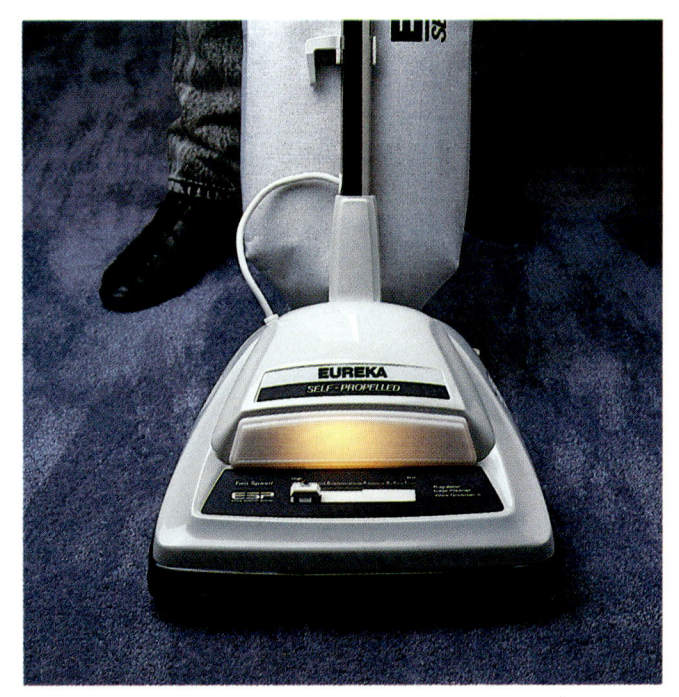

Choose a powerful vacuum sweeper such as this upright model to ensure deep-down carpet cleaning power. Grit in carpet fibers causes premature wear.

Repairing Carpeting

Stains and burns are the most common carpeting problems. If you cannot remove a stain, you usually can patch the carpeting by cutting away the damaged area and inserting a new piece of carpet. With superficial burns, clip away burned fibers with a fingernail scissors.

Another common problem is carpet seams or edges that have come loose. You can rent tools for fixing all of the problems shown on these pages.

Before You Start:

Tools & Materials: cookie-cutter carpet tool, double-face tape, knee kicker, seam adhesive, heat-activated tape, seam iron.

How to Repair Burned or Stained Carpeting

1 Remove extensive damage or stain with "cookie-cutter" tool, available at carpeting stores. Press cutter down over damaged area and twist to cut away carpet.

2 Cut replacement patch from scrap carpeting using cookie cutter. Insert double-face carpet tape under carpet so that tape overlaps patch seam.

3 Press patch into place. Make sure direction of nap or pattern matches existing carpet. Seal seam with seam adhesive to prevent unraveling.

92

How to Restretch Loose Carpeting

1 Adjust head of knee kicker so that prongs reach through to carpet backing. Press head of kicker into carpet about 2 inches from wall.

2 Press firmly with knee to stretch carpeting over and down onto tackless strip. Tuck carpeting over strip with putty knife. If necessary, trim excess carpeting. Carpet backing is held by points on strip.

How to Reglue Loose Seams

1 Remove old tape from under carpet seam. Cut new heat-activated carpet tape to fit seam. Place tape under carpeting so that both carpet edges overlap tape.

2 Seal seam using a rented seam iron. Run heated iron along tape under carpeting to activate glue. As iron moves along, press down on seam to seal edges of carpet.

Repairing Vinyl Floorcovering

Deep scratches or tears in vinyl floorcoverings can usually be repaired if you have a patch that matches the damaged vinyl. Patterned floorcoverings like simulated brick or stone are easy to repair, because the edges of the patch are concealed by the pattern. If necessary, remove vinyl from a hidden area to use as patch material.

> **Before You Start:**
>
> Tools & Materials: scrap floorcovering, masking tape, carpenter's square, utility knife, putty knife, odorless mineral spirits, floorcovering adhesive, roller (rolling pin will do).
>
> Tip: When selecting new floorcovering, select true inlaid material, usually sold in 6-foot wide rolls. It is heavier and much more resistant to wear and damage than lighter vinyls.

How to Repair Vinyl Floorcovering

1 Select scrap vinyl that matches existing floor. Place the scrap over the damaged area and adjust it until the pattern matches. Tape the patch to the floor.

2 Use carpenter's square to outline patch. Draw along pattern lines to conceal patch seams. Use utility knife to cut through both layers of vinyl. Lift out damaged vinyl with a putty knife.

3 Apply mineral spirits to dissolve adhesive, then scrape clean with a putty knife or razor scraper. Apply new adhesive to patch, then fit patch into hole. Use roller on vinyl to ensure good bond. Wipe away excess adhesive.

Replacing Vinyl Floor Tiles

Replace individual floor tiles when they become buckled, cracked, or when they are badly stained. If you cannot find replacement tiles at a home center, remove a tile from a hidden area, inside a closet or behind a kitchen appliance.

Older tiles made of asphalt may have asbestos fibers in the backing. Because asbestos poses a health risk, have a professional replace the floorcovering.

Before You Start:

Tools & Materials: heat gun, odorless mineral spirits, putty knife, replacement floor tile, floor-covering adhesive, notched trowel, roller (rolling pin will do).

Tip: If you do not have a heat gun, try setting a pan of ice cubes over the tile. The cold makes the tile adhesive brittle, allowing the tile to pop up easily.

How to Replace Vinyl Floor Tiles

1 Use a heat gun to heat tile and soften underlying adhesive. Be careful not to melt tile. Lift tile out with putty knife.

2 Apply mineral spirits to dissolve floorcovering adhesive. Scrape away all adhesive with putty knife or razor scraper.

3 Apply adhesive to underlayment. Position tile in hole. Use roller on tile to ensure a good bond. Wipe away excess adhesive.

Repairing Hardwood Floors

Repair scratches and holes in hardwood floors with a latex wood patch (available in various wood tones), and remove stains with oxalic acid, available at home centers or paint stores. For routine cleaning and renewing, choose a hardwood floor kit containing wood cleaner, restorer and application cloth.

Give hardwood a coat of protective wax/cleaner twice yearly to guard against scratches and water damage. Always use solvent-type cleaners on hardwood: water-base cleaners can blacken wood.

Before You Start:

Tools & Materials: wood patch, putty knife, sandpaper, wood restorer, rubber gloves, oxalic acid, vinegar, wood cleaner, combination wax/cleaner.

Tip: If your floors have excessive wax buildup, strip them with odorless mineral spirits, then rewax with a solvent-type wax/cleaner.

How to Patch Hardwood Floors

1 Apply a latex wood patch to fill in the scratches, staple marks or nail holes in hardwood floors.

2 Sand the wood patch smooth with fine sandpaper. Sand in the direction of wood grain.

3 Apply wood restorer with a clean cloth, and blend it into the existing finish.

How to Remove Stains from Hardwood Floors

1 Sand the stain area to remove old finish. Wearing rubber gloves, pour oxalic acid on stain and let stand for one hour to bleach stain. Repeat if necessary.

2 Rinse the stain area with vinegar. Let the wood dry completely.

3 Coat the bleached wood with a wood restorer. Apply several coats of restorer until the floor matches the old finish.

How to Clean & Renew Hardwood Floors

1 Vacuum hardwood floor to remove grit and dirt. Pour wood cleaner from kit on worn areas. When renewing an entire room, divide floor into 3 × 3-foot sections.

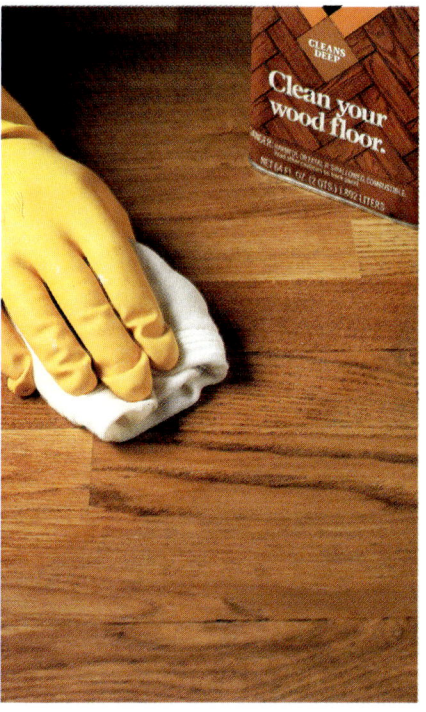

2 Rub over area with a dry cloth or fine steel wool. Let floor dry, then buff the wood by hand or with a buffing machine.

3 Apply a combination wax/cleaner or paste wax, then wax twice yearly for extra protection.

Silencing Squeaking Floors & Stairs

Floors and stairs squeak when wooden floor boards or structural beams rub against each other. The X-bridging (wood braces) between the joists can squeak when the floor above flexes under traffic. Floor boards may squeak if they have not been properly nailed to the subfloor. Water pipes or air ducts may also rub against floor joists.

When possible, fix squeaks from underneath the floor or staircase. If the floor or staircase is covered by a finished ceiling, work on squeaks from the top side. With hardwood floors, drive finish nails into the seams between planks to silence squeaking. With floors covered by carpeting or linoleum, fix squeaks when replacing the floorcovering.

Before You Start:

Tools & Materials: hammer, 1-inch wood screws, screwdriver or screwgun, carpenter's glue, hardwood wedges, construction adhesive; caulk gun, wood blocks, flooring nails, nail set.

Three Ways to Silence Squeaking Floors

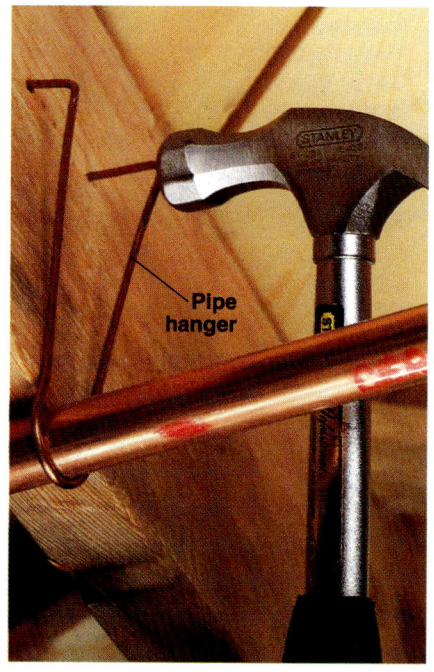

Check pipe hangers, heating ducts and X-bridging for rubbing. Loosen tight pipe hangers and separate wooden bridging to eliminate any rubbing.

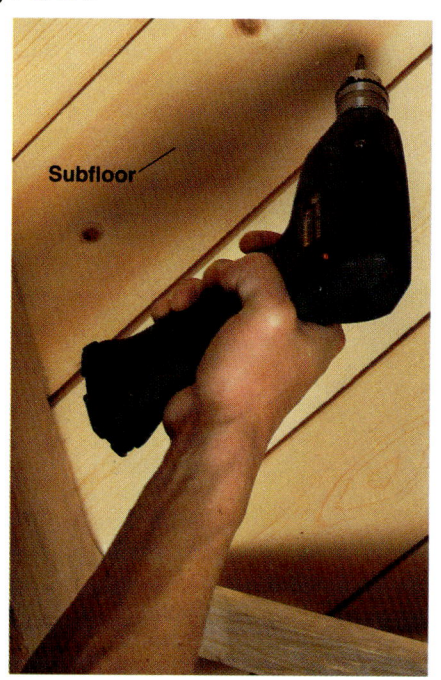

Drive wood screws to draw hardwood flooring and subfloor together and stop them from squeaking. Make certain screws are not too long. Use a screwgun to make this overhead task easier.

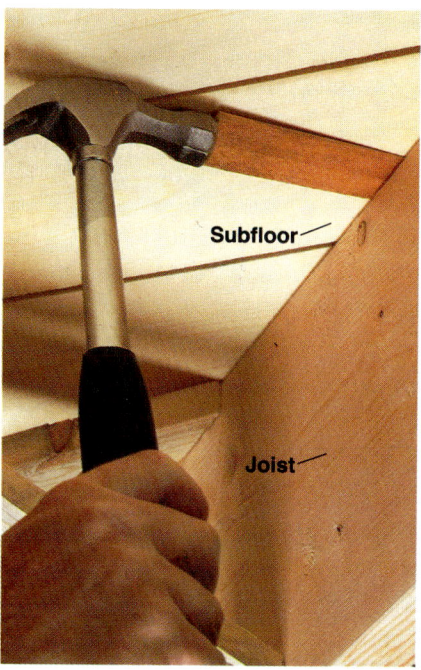

Cut hardwood wedges and drive the wedges between the joists and subfloor to prevent flexing of the floor.

Three Ways to Silence Squeaking Stairs

Glue wood blocks with construction adhesive underneath stairs to reinforce the joints between treads and risers. After gluing, secure the wood blocks with wood screws.

Cut hardwood wedges and coat them with carpenter's glue. Drive wedges between the treads and risers to tighten the joints and stop squeaks.

Anchor treads to risers by driving flooring nails at opposing angles to prevent loosening. With hardwood, drill pilot holes for nails. Use a nail set to recess nails, then putty nail holes.

99

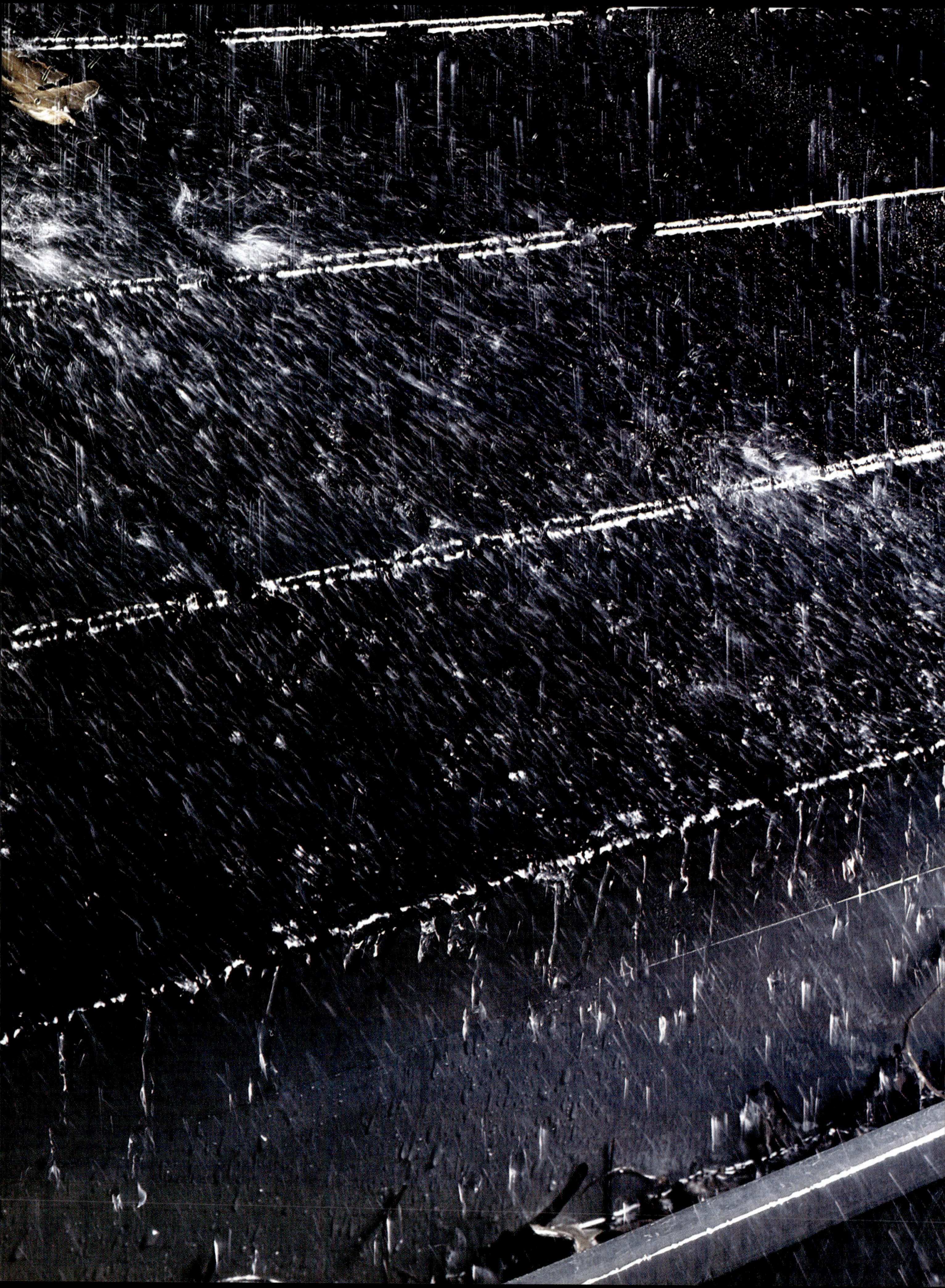

Roof & Exteriors

Exterior Home Repairs

The goal of most exterior home repairs is to keep your home weather-tight. Leaks in roofing or rain gutters can cause expensive damage to interior ceilings, insulation, furnishings and basements. Window and door frames will rot quickly if they are not periodically recaulked. Open cracks allow insects and pests to enter and cause enormous winter heat loss.

Check the exterior of your home regularly for signs of trouble. Curled and broken shingles and rusted metal flashings and rain gutters cause roof and basement leaks. Check for pools and puddles around the foundation during a rain: these also cause wet-basement problems.

Many exterior repairs require the use of a ladder. Use a ladder as directed by the manufacturer, and never exceed the ladder's weight rating. Note: Never use a ladder when it is raining.

Tips & Techniques for Ladder Safety

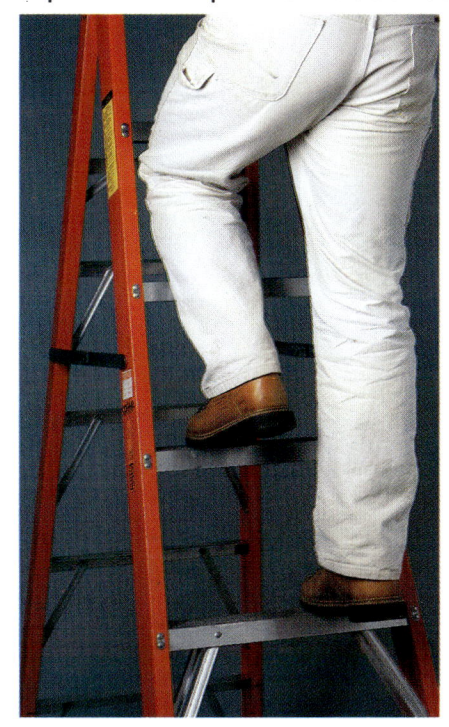

Center your weight on the ladder. Wear clothing such as blue jeans or painters' whites when climbing. Wear rubber-soled, over-the-ankle work shoes for safety and comfort.

Brace ladder before climbing, and read the manufacturer's sticker. Do not use the top shelf or rung as a foot support. Do not overreach when working: move the ladder instead.

Do not climb with your hands full of tools. Assemble all necessary tools and place them in a pail to be hoisted up.

Use cordless tools while climbing on roofs and ladders to avoid the hazard caused by loose tool or extension cords.

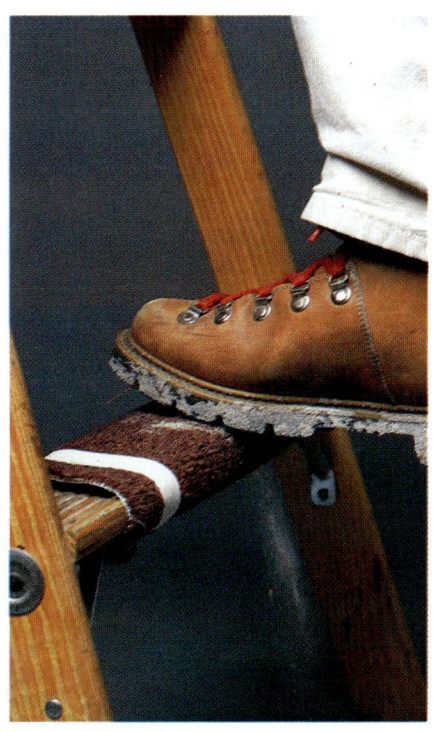

Tape scrap carpeting or burlap tightly around the bottom rung of a ladder. Wipe your shoes free of mud or sand to prevent slipping when climbing.

Anchor your ladder. Attach top rung to a short block of wood with rope. Open window, place block inside, and close window.

Fixing a Leaking Roof

Most roof leaks are caused by damaged or worn shingles, or by rusted metal flashings. Flashings line the roof deck wherever there is an interruption in the continuous roofline — such as in valleys, around roof dormers, or whenever skylights, chimneys or vent pipes cut through the roofing.

Ice dams caused by freezing water can back up under the shingles and cause interior water damage.

When you first see signs of ceiling wetness, try to locate the source of the leak and prevent further water damage. Roof leaks are not always found directly above the wet mark on your ceiling. Water can enter the attic and travel far down a rafter before dropping off onto the ceiling below. Wait for dry weather before examining the exterior roofing to find the cause of the leak.

Before You Start:

Tools & Materials: flashlight, hammer, nail, wood block, bucket, awl, pry bar, new shingles, galvanized roofing nails, roofing mastic, caulk gun, sandpaper, fiberglass repair kit, rusty-metal primer, rust-proof paint.

How to Locate a Leak & Minimize Water Damage

1 Check attic for water on rafters and sheathing. Place bucket under dripping water. Trace water to source of leaking, and mark the location.

2 If water flows down toward a wall, nail a small block of wood in the water trickle to direct dripping water into a bucket.

3 Minimize water damage to plaster or wallboard. Locate center of water stain on ceiling. Drive awl or nail into center of stain area to release water into a bucket.

How to Find the Cause of a Roof Leak

Shingles that are broken or curled are likely causes of roof leaks. If you spot a damaged shingle near the suspected location of a leak, replace the shingle, (page 108).

Metal flashings with rust damage can cause leaks. Flashings seal the roof wherever the roofline is interrupted: around roof vents, chimney, skylight or in valleys where the roofline changes. To correct the problem, repair the flashing (page 109).

Minimize Damage from Ice Dams

Prevent further ice backup by melting a channel through the ice with hot water. This allows water to flow off the roof before it freezes. Or call a professional to thaw and remove ice dams using steam equipment.

Prevent ice dams by improving ventilation and insulation in the attic. Adding ventilation prevents the build-up of heated air which can melt snow on the roof. If the attic is inaccessible, call a professional.

Emergency Roof Repairs

Use a sheet of plywood for an emergency roof cover. Use double-headed nails to temporarily secure the plywood. Patch the nail holes with roof mastic after you remove the nails.

Use plastic sheeting or a tarp to provide emergency cover to a roof after a damaging storm. Hold the edges of the plastic down with nailed strips of lath until roof can be fixed. Patch the nail holes with roof mastic after you remove the nails.

Roof Maintenance Tips

Limbs overhanging roof contribute to moss buildup, and can cause wear to the shingles.

Cut limbs with pruning saw to prevent wear of roofing material, and to increase sunlight. Added sunlight dries roof deck to prevent moss and mildew.

Moss or mildew on a roof deck is caused by too much shade, and by twigs and leaves that block drainage between the shingles. Moss or mildew can cause deterioration in the roofing material.

Power wash the roof deck with a pressure sprayer to eliminate moss and remove twigs and leaves.

Nail zinc strip with sealing roofing nails along the center ridge of shingled roofs to prevent moss buildup. Zinc washes down roof deck during each rain, killing the moss and mildew.

Detect Roof Wear

Curled or cracked shingles caused by years of exposure to the elements are likely to cause roof leaks. Check roof from the ground using binoculars.

Gravel in downspouts or rain gutters indicates that the surface of the shingles is wearing away. Roofing may need to be replaced soon.

How to Replace Shingles

1 Raise the edge of the damaged shingle. Use a slim pry bar to remove nails holding shingle. Remove damaged shingle.

2 Insert new shingle and align it with adjacent shingles. Peel away the liner that covers the adhesive on back of the shingle.

3 Drive galvanized roofing nails near each side and at the top of each slot on the new shingle. Nail heads should be covered by overlapping shingles.

4 Dab roofing mastic over each nail head and press shingles flat. The sun's heat will activate adhesive and seal down the shingle.

How to Repair Flashing

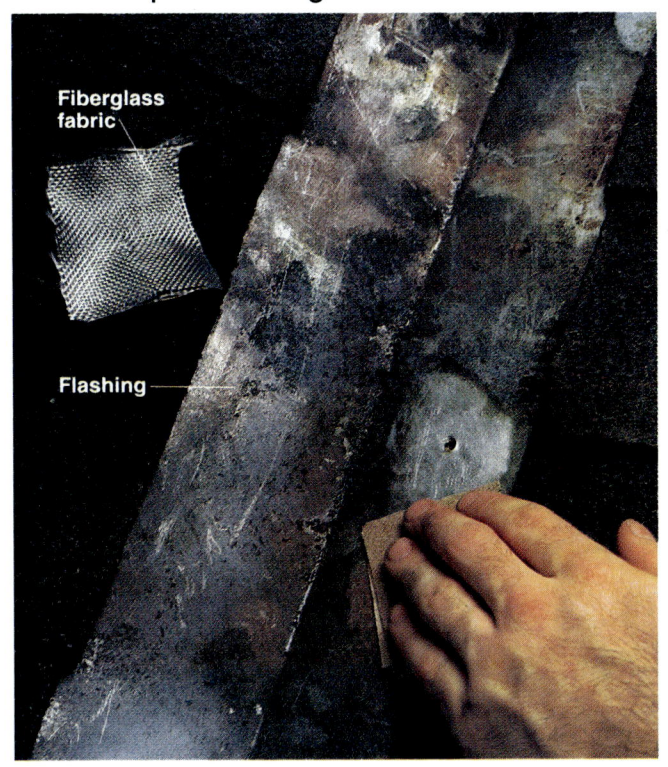

1 Sand metal flashing. Patch rust holes with an automotive fiberglass mending kit, following manufacturer's directions.

2 Let the fiberglass application harden, then apply several additional coats of resin over the patch, if needed. Let resin set hard.

3 Sand patch area and any additional rust spots. Apply a coat of rusty-metal primer to all sanded areas. Let primer dry, then repaint patched flashing with a finish coat of rust-proof paint.

4 Caulk all edges where shingles and flashing meet with a bead of roofing mastic.

Downspout & Gutter Problems & Repairs

Ninety-five percent of all wet basement problems occur because water pools near the foundation. To prevent the problem, fix downspouts and gutters so that rain falling on the roof runs well away from the foundation.

Four Common Problems Caused by Faulty Downspouts & Gutters

Wet basements can cause damage to furnishings, appliances and floorcoverings. Wet basements can usually be traced to roof gutters and downspouts that are plugged, rusted through, or are not diverted away from the house. To correct the problem, fix downspouts and gutters (pages 112, 114), and check the slope of the earth around the foundation (page 113).

Peeling paint on basement walls is caused by moisture in the wall behind the paint. This is usually caused by water seeping through the wall from the outside. To correct the problem, fix the downspouts and gutters (pages 112, 114), and check the slope of the earth around the foundation (page 113).

110

After checking and fixing downspouts and gutters, check the soil grade around the house, and, if necessary, create a slight downhill slope away from the walls.

Before You Start:

Tools & Materials: trowel, garden hose, mesh leaf guard, carpenter's level, sandpaper or paint scraper, replacement gutter section, roof mastic, fiberglass repair kit, rusty-metal primer, rust-proof paint, hacksaw, ground pipe extension.

Stained walls and fascias are often caused by roof gutters that leak or overflow. Gutters overflow if they are plugged with leaves and debris. To correct the problem, fix downspouts and gutters (pages 112, 114), and check the slope of the earth around the foundation (page 113).

Puddles on walkways will cause the concrete to deteriorate. Icy sidewalks are dangerous, and wherever dripping water causes ice on sidewalks, there is also a danger of falling icicles. To correct the problem, fix downspouts and gutters (pages 112, 114), check the slope of the slab (page 113), and repair and seal concrete (pages 122-123).

How to Unplug Gutters & Downspouts

1 Clean leaves, twigs and other material out of rain gutters using a trowel. Debris in gutters can hold moisture and cause galvanized gutters to rust.

2 Flush out the debris by inserting a garden hose into the downspout, and turning on the water. Check for rust in gutters, and repair any holes (page 114).

Check slope of gutters with a level. Gutters should angle toward downspouts. Water that stands in gutters can cause metal to rust.

Shield gutters with a mesh leaf guard to prevent clogs in the downspouts. Leaves are washed over gutters during rain.

How to Check & Correct a Foundation Grade

1 Tape a carpenter's level to a straight 8-foot-long 2 × 4 board, and check the grade around the house. If the earth around the foundation is level, standing water can seep into the basement.

2 Add soil around the foundation to increase the grade away from the foundation. Rake the soil smooth, and recheck the slope.

Ground pipe

3 For proper grade, the outside end of the 2 × 4 should be at least 6" above the ground when the 2 × 4 is level. Add a ground pipe to deliver water at least 6 to 8 feet from the foundation (page 115). Plant grass right up to the foundation to help shed water.

Concrete slabs such as walks or patios should slope away from the house. If slab is level or slopes toward foundation, consider having it raised by "mud-jacking." Look under Concrete Contractors in your Yellow Pages for a contractor who offers this service.

How to Repair a Leaking Gutter

1 Scrape away any peeling paint and rust, using sandpaper or scraper. Patch holes with a section of matching gutter. Use a fiberglass repair kit to patch other rusty areas.

2 Cut a section of matching gutter to cover gutter areas that are rusted through. Apply roof mastic to patch area, then press patch firmly in place.

3 For other rusty areas, brush fiberglass resin on metal. Cover resin with fiberglass fabric cut to fit gutter. Let resin harden slightly, then brush on more. Let resin dry overnight.

4 Coat all repair areas with a rusty-metal primer. Let primer dry, then repaint patched gutters with finish coat of rust-proof paint.

How to Extend Downspouts

1 Water pooling near foundation can cause a wet basement. Begin by checking the slope of the foundation grade (page 113).

2 Use a hacksaw to cut a section of downspout that is 6 to 8 feet long.

3 Attach the pipe to the downspout with a galvanized elbow.

4 Place a splash block at the end of the ground pipe to disperse water onto the lawn.

115

Filling Cracks & Holes

Caulks block air movement and help conserve energy. They also prevent water, dirt and pests from entering.

A wide variety of modern caulks are available to fill cracks and holes in wood, masonry, concrete and blacktop. Fill large gaps in foundations and siding with fiberglass insulation to form a base for the caulk. Large gaps in masonry should be filled with new mortar.

Before You Start:

Tools & Materials: tube caulks, utility knife, caulk gun, fiberglass insulation, smoothing tool (plastic spoon or flat stick), masonry chisel, ball peen hammer, mortar, pointed trowel, joint tool, muriatic acid.

Tip: Keep a bowl of cold water handy and dip the smoothing tool (or your fingertip) to avoid smearing latex caulk. Clean up butyl or oil-base caulks with mineral spirits.

Types of caulk include (clockwise from top left): peel-and-stick caulk, roofing mastic, butyl-base caulk, acrylic latex caulk, butyl driveway patcher, latex masonry patcher, clear weatherproofing caulk.

How to Use a Caulk Gun

1 Cut off tip of caulk tube to the desired bead size. Some caulk tubes have trimming guides on the tip.

2 Insert a long nail to break seal on tube. Insert tube into caulk gun and push the plunger against the base of caulk tube.

3 Hold the gun at an angle and squeeze trigger evenly while caulking. Draw tip of caulk tube steadily to apply an even bead.

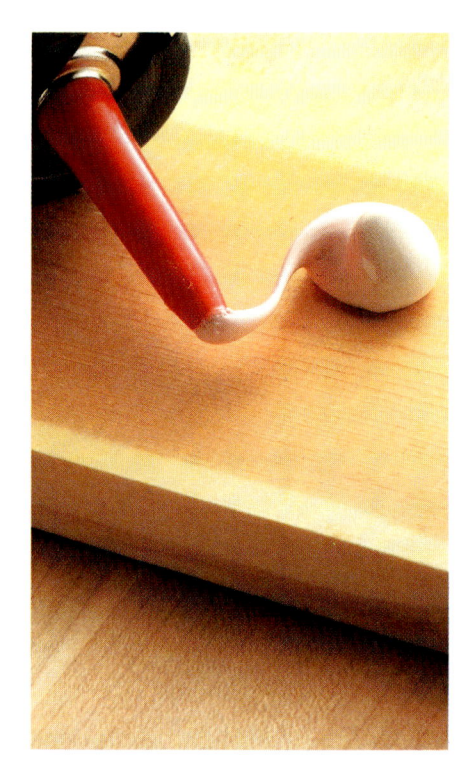

4 Set caulk tube on scrap wood, and pull plunger back to avoid drips. Wipe excess caulk from tip. Cover tip to prevent the tube from drying out.

Dip a flat stick in water and use it to smooth a latex caulk bead in locations where appearance is important.

A wet finger can also be used to smooth a latex or silicone caulk bead. Keep water handy to rinse caulk and moisten finger.

Tips for Sealing Holes & Cracks in Exterior Walls

Caulk windows and doors with a good-quality latex or silicone caulk. Caulking prevents moisture from rotting the wood, and reduces heat loss.

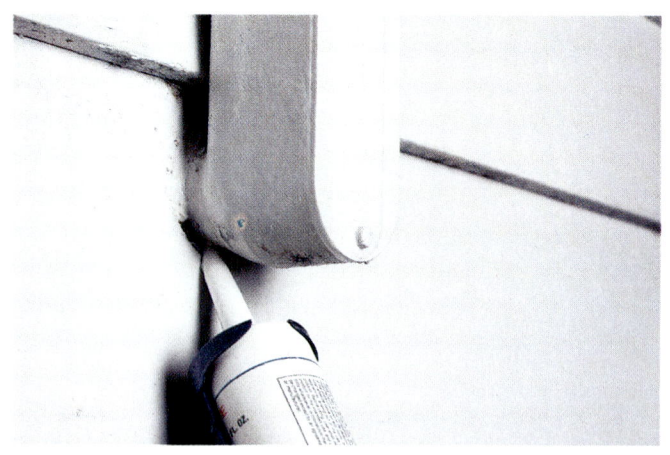

Caulk around wires and pipes entering the house. Remove old, cracked caulk before applying new, colored caulk that matches siding.

Caulk mud sill, the horizontal wooden plate where the house rests on the foundation. This should be periodically recaulked to prevent heat loss.

Stuff fiberglass insulation into large holes and cracks to provide a base for the caulk. Fiberglass also insulates.

Caulk under shingles with a good-quality roof mastic.

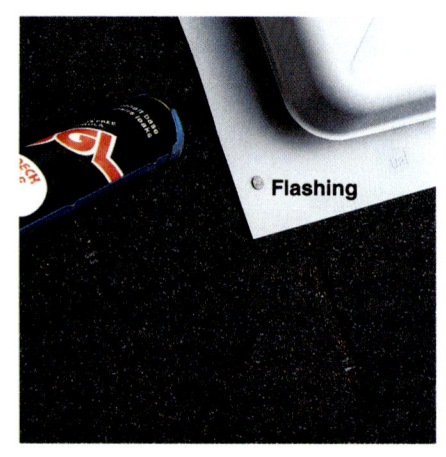

Caulk roof flashings around chimneys, vents and skylights with roof mastic to protect against water entry.

Coat nailheads with roof mastic to prevent leaks after replacing roof shingles.

How to Fill Masonry Cracks

1 Remove loose masonry with a masonry chisel and wire brush. Clean surfaces with brush or hand vacuum.

2 Use a caulk gun to apply masonry patch to crack. Latex masonry fillers are easy to apply and clean up.

3 Smooth the masonry caulk with a putty knife, trowel, or with a wooden dowel.

How to Replace Mortar

1 Chip out loose mortar with a masonry chisel and ball peen hammer. Clean cracks with a wire brush or hand vacuum.

2 Mix fresh mortar and apply to cracks with a pointed trowel.

3 Smooth mortar with a smoothing tool or round wooden dowel. Let mortar dry overnight.

4 Clean brick face with a brush and a 5% muriatic acid solution, available at home centers. Wear protective clothes when working with acid.

Concrete Repairs

Concrete can be broken or chipped, stained by rust or oil, or cracked by the effects of water — the chief enemy of concrete. Keep the concrete slab well sealed, and repair soil erosion around the slab to prevent water from getting underneath.

Pop-ups are conical holes in concrete, caused by expansion of a rock chip at the base of the hole.

Cracks in concrete are caused by expansion and contraction of the slab. This is caused by temperature changes, or by water washing away the gravel base.

Chipped corners on steps are usually caused by a blow with a heavy object.

Stains on concrete can occur when the surface is not sealed. Seal concrete with a clear masonry sealer once each year for maximum protection against staining and water damage.

> **Before You Start:**
>
> Tools & Materials: muriatic acid, rubber gloves, eye protection, trisodium phosphate (TSP), squeegee/broom or paint roller, masonry chisel, ball peen hammer, powdered concrete patcher with bonding liquid, trowel, caulk-type concrete patcher.
>
> Tip: Repair concrete when temperature is 50° to 80°F and winds are light. Concrete will not set properly if it dries too fast, or if it freezes while wet.

Tools for Concrete ▶

Squeegee/broom

Trowels & joint tools

Masonry chisel

How to Clean & Seal Concrete

1 Clean concrete with brush and a 5% solution of muriatic acid, available at home centers. Wear gloves and protective clothes when working with acid.

2 Flush the surface with TSP (tri-sodium phosphate) solution, then rinse with hose or high-pressure power washer.

3 Apply concrete sealer with a paint roller, squeegee or garden sprayer.

How to Repair Chipped Concrete Steps

1 Clean chipped concrete with a wire brush. Brush patch area with latex bonding liquid.

2 Mix concrete patcher with water, then stir in bonding liquid, as directed by manufacturer. Apply to patch area with flexible knife or trowel.

3 Tape scrap lumber pieces around corner of step, as shown, to hold the patch until it hardens.

How to Patch Pop-ups & Cracks in Concrete

1 Chip out rocks at bottom of pop-up hole with a masonry chisel and hammer. Wear goggles to avoid eye injury.

2 Remove dirt and debris from hole with a shop vacuum. If hole contains oil or grease, wash with a detergent, then rinse with water.

3 Coat the edges of the hole with a latex bonding liquid. Mix concrete with water, then stir in bonding liquid. Pour in the mixture, and smooth with a flexible knife or trowel.

Cracks between a concrete walk and foundation can cause a wet basement. Repair cracks with caulk-type concrete patcher.

Asphalt Care & Repair

Asphalt blacktop driveways and walks can be damaged by impact or by water penetration. Water running under blacktop from the side or through cracks will undermine the gravel base that cushions the slab. To repair asphalt and prevent serious damage, fill holes and cracks with asphalt patcher, seal the surface, and fill washouts along the slab edge to prevent water from entering.

Before You Start:

Tools & Materials: garden hose, vacuum, heat gun, trowel, asphalt cleaner, caulk gun, asphalt patcher, putty knife, asphalt sealer, squeegee/broom.

Tip: Wait for a warm, sunny day to seal asphalt.

How to Patch Holes in Asphalt

1 Remove dirt and debris from hole with a shop vacuum. Flush the hole with a garden hose and spray nozzle.

2 Pour asphalt patching material into the hole. Warm patch material with heat gun. Level and smooth the patch with a trowel.

3 Tamp patching material so it is firmly packed in hole. Firm, smooth patches prevent future water damage.

How to Seal an Asphalt Drive

1 Fill any holes in slab (page opposite). Clean slab with asphalt-cleaning product to remove oil and dirt from surface. Rinse slab with hose or power washer.

2 Patch cracks in asphalt using caulk gun and a tube of asphalt patcher. Large cracks may need several applications.

3 Spread and smooth the patch material using a putty knife. Dip scraper in cold water or mineral spirits to prevent the patcher from sticking to scraper.

4 Pour a pool of sealer on the slab and spread it following manufacturer's directions. Too thick a layer will not cure properly. It is better to apply two coats.

5 Allow sealer to cure well before driving or walking on it. Block drive with sawhorses or rope and ladders to prevent traffic during the drying period.

Index

sponge, 8
synthetic bristle, 8
Butyl-base caulk, 116

C

Cams and cam washers, ball-type faucets, 17, 19
Carbide masonry drill bit, 86
Carpenter's square, 9, 94
Carpeting, 91-93
burns or stains, 92
edge trimmers, 91
on ladders, 103
regluing and restretching, 93
seam tape, 92-93
Cartridge faucets, 16-21
disc-type, 16, 17, 20
replacement parts, 17
sleeve-type, 16, 17, 21
Cartridge fuses, 38
Caulk gun, 117
Caulking, 116-119
asphalt care and repair, 124-125
bathtub or shower stall, 89
concrete patching, 123
exterior cracks or holes, 116-119
flashings, 109, 118
masonry cracks, 119
mud sills, 118
shingles, 118
windows and doors, 118
wires and pipes, 118
Ceilings, 73-79
cleaning stains, 74-75
hanging objects, 76-79
Center punch, 9
Ceramic tile, 86-89
Channel-type pliers, 6
Chemical root remover, 28, 31
Chisels, 6, 8, 121
Circuit breakers, 38
Circuit map, 40
Circuit testers, 36, 38-39, 47-50
Circular saw, 7, 9
Clamps, 8
Claw hammer, 9
Cleanout plug, main drain, 31
Clevis assembly, pop-up sink drain stopper, 32
Clogs, plumbing repairs, 14, 28, 33
Closet auger, drains, 15, 33
CO/ALR wire rating, 39
Combination tool, electrical repair, 37, 41
Compression faucet, 16, 17, 22-23
Concrete, 120-122
caulking, 116-119
cleaning and sealing, 122
damage, 111
foundation grading, 113
repairs, 120-123
stains, 120, 122
Continuity tester, 37
lamp cord problems, 45
light fixture, 51
wall switch, 49
Cookie cutter carpet tool, 91-92
Copper sulfate root remover, 28, 31
Cord plug replacement, 42-43
Cordless tools, safety tips, 103
Cracks and holes,
caulking, 116-119
concrete, 120-123

D

Deep socket, ratchet, 15
Diaphragm ballcock, 14, 27
Dimmer switch, 49
Disc-type cartridge faucet, 16, 20
Dome cap, 20
Doors, 53-71
bifold, 55
caulking, 118
cleaning and lubricating, 54-55
garage, 55
latch repairs, 68-69
lockset repair, 66-67
mats, 91
removing, 70
screens, 64-65
sliding, 55
sticking, 70-71
sweeps, 56-57
warped, 68-69
weatherstripping, 56-59
Double-hung windows, 60-63
Downspouts, 110-112
extending, 115
Drain(s), 14, 28-32
auger, 15, 28, 30
plunger, 29
stopper, 29, 32
trap, 30-31
Drain-waste-vent lines, 14
Drapes, hanging, 78-79
Drills, 7, 9-10
Drivable wall anchor, 78
Driveways,
care and repair, 124-125
patching caulk, 116

E

Electrical repairs, 35-51
connections, 41-43
light fixture, 44-45, 50-51
receptacle replacement, 46-47
safety, 38-39
wall switch, 48-49
Electricity, shut-off, 38
Electronic stud finder, 77
Escutcheon, 23
Expansion nozzle, drain clogs, 15, 29
Exterior repairs, 102-125
asphalt care, 124-125
concrete repairs, 120-121
cracks and holes, 116-119
leaking roof, 104-109

F

Faceplate, locksets, 66-68
Fascias, 111
Fasteners, walls and ceilings, 78-79
Faucet(s), 16-23
ball-type, 14, 16, 17, 19
cartridge, 14, 16-21
compression, 16, 17, 22-23
disc-type, 16, 20
replacing, 18
sleeve-type, 16, 21
wall-mounted, 23
Fiberglass,
insulation, 118

A

Adhesive,
ceramic tile, 87
floorcovering, 95
vinyl v-stripping, 56, 58-59
wallcovering, 84
wallhanger hook, 78
Adjustable wrench, 6, 16
Allen wrench, 15-16
Aluminum-frame screens, 65
Asphalt care and repair, 124-125
Attic, ventilation and insulation, 106
Auger, 15, 33
Awl, 6

B

Ball peen hammer, 31
Ballcock, 14, 24-27
Ball-type faucets, 14, 17, 19
Basements, moisture in, 110
Bathtub, caulking, 89
Bifold doors, lubrication and adjustment, 55
Bits, drill, 7
Blacktop,
caulking, 116
repair, 124-125
Blow bag for clogged drains, 29
Bonnet nut, wall-mounted compression faucet, 23
Brad pusher, 11
Branch drain, 28, 30
Brown coat, plaster wall, 77
Brushes,
natural bristle, 8

126

joint tape, 74
repair fabric, 109, 114
resin, 114
self-adhesive tape, 82
wallboard tape, 81
window screen fabric, 64-65
Files, 6, 8
Finish coat, plaster walls, 77
Fixtures,
electrical light, 50-51
tile, hanging, 86
Flanged plunger, 15, 33
Flapper valve, toilets, 14, 24-26
Flashings, roofing, 104-105, 109, 118
Flat-cord plug, 42
Float, toilets, 24-27
arm, 26
ball, 24-25
cup, 26, 27
rod, 25
Floor drains, 28-29
Floorcovering adhesive, 95
Floors, 90-99
burn or stain removal, 91, 96-97
carpet repair, 92-93
hardwood, 96-97
squeaks, 98-99
vinyl floorcovering, 94-95
Flush problems, toilets, 24-27
Foundation grade, 113
Freshwater supply pipes, 14
Fuses, 38

G

Garage door openers, 55
Garage doors, 55-57
Glass, replacing, 62-63
Glazing compound, 63
Glazing points, 54, 62-63
Glue gun, 9, 75, 81
Graphite lubricant, 54
Grip-It™ screw anchor, 78-79
Ground pipe, 113, 115
Ground system, 38
Ground wires, 38, 42-43
Ground-fault circuit interrupter (GFCI), 39, 46
receptacle replacement, 46-47
Grout, 86-88
Grout float, 75, 88
Guide arm, 26
Guide disc, 23
Gum eraser, 84
Gutters, 107, 110-114

H

Hacksaw, 6, 15, 115
Hammer, 6, 9
Hand saw, 6
Hardwood, 96-99
clean and renew, 97
predrilling, 11
squeaks, 99
stain removal, 96-97
wedges, 99
Heat gun, 54, 63, 75, 91, 95
Heat-activated carpet tape, 91, 93
Heatproof grease, faucet repair, 16
Hinges, door repairs, 70-71
Holes and cracks, caulking 116-119
Hot glue gun, 9
Hot wires, 36

I

Ice dams, 104, 106
Index cap, faucets, 20-21, 22
Insulating sleeve, lamp sockets, 45
Insulation, 106, 118

J

Jig saw, 7, 9
Joint tools, 121
Joists, 77, 98-99

K

Keys, plaster walls, 77
Knee kicker, 91, 93

L

Ladders, safety tips, 103
Lamp socket replacement, 44-45
Latchbolt, 67-69
Latex,
bonding liquid, 82-83, 122-123
caulk, 89, 116-118
glazing, 63
masonry patcher, 116
wood patch, 96
Lath,
rock, 77
wood, 77
Leaf guard, 112
Leaking roof, 104-109
Leaks, plumbing, 14, 16-23
Levels, 8, 112-113
Lift chain or wires, toilets, 24
Light bulbs, broken, 40
Light fixtures, 50-51
Lockset, 54, 66-67
Lubrication, windows and doors, 54-55, 60, 66-68, 70

M

Magnetic stud finder, 75, 77
Main drain, 28, 31
Main service panel, 36, 37
Masonry,
anchor plug, plastic or lead, 86
filling cracks, 116, 119
Mastic, roofing, 108-109
Measurement techniques, 9, 18
Metal weatherstripping, 56, 59
Mirror clips, 78-79
Mirrors, hanging, 78-79
Molly bolt, 78
Mortar, replacing, 119
Moss or mildew, roof damage, 107
Mud sills, 118
Mud-jacking, 113
Muriatic acid, concrete repair, 119, 122

N

Nail(s), 11
coating with mastic, 118
galvanized roofing, 11, 108
pops in wallboard, 80
set, 11
stud locations, 77
Nailed picture hanger, 78
Needlenose pliers, 6
Neon circuit tester, 36-37, 39
Neutral wires, 36

O

O-rings, plumbing, 16-17, 19, 21-23
Outlets, 39, 46-47
Overflow plate, 32
Overflow tube, toilets, 25

P

Packing string and washers, plumbing, 22
Paint,
film on stuck window, 60
peeling, 110
solvent, 54
spatters, 74
Paint zipper, 54, 60-61
Passage locksets, 66-67
Paste wax for hardwood floors, 97
Patching holes, wallboard, 80-81
Patching tape, 72, 81-82
Peel-and-stick caulk, 89, 116
Picture hangers, nailed, 78
Pilot hole, 10
Pipe hangers, squeaking floor, 99
Pipes,
caulking around, 118
draining, 14
Pivot blocks, bifold doors, 55
Plants, hanging from ceiling, 78-79
Plaster repair, 77, 82-83
Plastic anchors, hanging mirrors, 78-79
Plastic sheeting, emergency roof cover, 106
Pliers, 6, 15-16, 30-31, 37, 40
Plugs, 39, 42-43
flat-cord, 42-43
polarized, 39
quick-connect, 42-43
round-cord, 42-43
three-prong, 39
Plumbing, 13-33
Plunger, clogged drains, 15, 29, 33
Plunger valve ballcock, toilets, 14, 27
Plywood as emergency roof cover, 106
Polarized plugs, 39
Popped nails, 80
Pop-up sink drain stopper, 29, 32
Pop-ups, concrete repairs, 120, 123
Power tools, 7
Power wash, 107
Protective caps, 39
Pry bar, 6
Pull chain socket, 44
Pull rod, 26
Push lever socket, 44
Putty knife, 6, 54, 63

Q

Quick-connect plug, electrical repair, 41-43

R

Ratings, electrical, 39, 49, 51
Razor scraper, 91

127

Receptacles, 38-39, 46-47
  GFCI, 46
  grounded three-prong, 38, 46
  protective caps, 39
  replacing, 46-47
  two-prong, 38-39, 46
Refill tube, 25
Regrouting ceramic tile, 88
Remote switch socket, 44
Riser, 99
Rock lath, 77
Roofing mastic, 108-109, 116, 118
Roofs, 101-109
  leaking, 104-106
  maintenance, 107
  overhanging limbs, 107
  repairs, emergency, 106
Root remover, 28, 31
Rotating ball, 19
Round-cord plug, 43
Rusty-metal primer, 109, 114

S

Safety, 5
  childproof receptacle caps, 39
  electrical repairs, 36, 38-41
  ladders, 103
Sanding, 6-7, 71
Sash brush, 75
Sash cords, 60-61
Saws, 6-7, 9
Screens, 64-65
Screw anchor, 78-79
Screw terminal connection, 41
Screwdrivers, 6, 8, 10, 37
Screws, 10
Sealer,
  asphalt, 125
  concrete, 122
  door warping, 69
  wood, 63
Seals, 16
  neoprene, 21
Seam iron, 91-93
Seat wrench, 15-16, 23
Seat-dressing tool, 15-16, 23
Security locks, 67
Service panels, electrical, 36-37
Shellac, 74, 83
Shimming doors, 69
Shingles,
  caulking, 118
  replacing, 105, 107-108
Short circuit, 38
Shower drain, 29
Shower stall, caulking, 89
Shutoff valves, 14
Sidelighting stud location, 77
Silicone caulk, 89, 117-118
Silicone spray lubricant, 54
Single-pole switches, 48
Sinks,
  clogs, 28-31
  drain stoppers, 32
Sleeve-type cartridge faucet, 21
Sliding windows and doors, 54-55
Socket-switch units, 44-45
Soil stack, 28
Solvent/lubricant, 54-55
Spindle, lockset repair, 67
Splash block, downspouts, 115
Spline, screen repair, 54, 65
Sponge brushes, 8
Spouts, 14, 18

Spring metal door stripping, 56-57
Spring-loaded windows, 60, 63
Square, 6, 9, 81
Squeegee/broom, 121
Stain removal,
  carpeting, 92
  hardwood floors, 91, 96-97
  walls and ceilings, 74-75
Stairs,
  concrete, 122
  squeaks, 98-99
Stem and seat compression faucet, 22
Steps, concrete repair, 122
Strike plate, lockset repairs, 68-69
Strip gauge, electrical connections, 41
Studs, 77
Sub floor, 68, 98-99
Sub panel, 37
Switches, electrical repairs, 48-49

T

Tack hammer, 11
Tackless strip, carpeting, 91
Tank ball, toilet repairs, 24-26
Tape measure, 6, 9
Tarp, emergency roof cover, 106
Tester, electrical circuits, 38-39, 49-50
Three-prong receptacle, 38-39, 46-47
Three-way switches, 48-49
Threshold, 56
Thumb latch, 67
Tile,
  ceramic, 86-89
  vinyl flooring, 95
Toenailing, 11
Toggle bolts, 78-79
Toilet(s),
  flush adjustment, 24
  repairs, 24-27, 33
  running, 24-25
Tool kit, 6
Tools, 6-9
  concrete, 121
  cordless, 103
  electrical, 37
  flooring, 91
  plumbing, 15
  walls and ceilings, 75
  windows and doors, 54
Tophat diaphragm and stem, faucets, 22
Tracks, cleaning and lubricating, 54-55
Trap, drains, 28, 30-33
Treads, 99
Tree roots, main drain, 31
Trip lever, toilets, 24, 29
Trisodium phosphate (TSP), 122
Trowels, concrete repairs, 121
Tub stopper, cleaning and adjusting, 32
Twist anchor, hanging drapes, 78-79
Twist-knob socket, 44

U

Underwriter's knot, 40, 43

V

Valve seats, plumbing, 14, 23
  dressing, 23
  replacing, 23

Valves, plumbing, 14, 16, 23
Ventilation, attic, 106
Vinegar, stain removal, 97
Vinyl floorcovering, 94-95
Vinyl weatherstripping, 56, 58-59

W

Walkways, ice damage, 111
Wall(s), 74-89
  anchor, 78
  cleaning, 74-75
  downspout/gutter stains, 110-111
  fastening objects to, 76-79
  holes and cracks in exterior, 118-119
Wall hangers, 74, 78-79
Wall switch replacement, 48-49
Wallboard, 77, 80-81
Wallboard twist anchor, 78
Wallcovering, 75, 84-85
Wall-mounted faucet, 23
Wallpaper dough, 84
Warped doors, 68-69
Washers, 14, 16, 17, 22-23
Water and electrical repair safety, 40
Water closet, 24, 25
Water damage, leaking roofs, 104-105
Water shutoff, 14
Wax/cleaner for hardwood floors, 97
Weatherproofing, 100, 116
  cleaning and lubricating, 54
Weatherstripping, 56-59
Weight pocket, 61
Wet sander, wallboard patching, 81
Windows, 53-67
  caulking, 118
  cleaning and lubricating, 54, 55
  loose or sticking, 60-61
  replacing glass, 62-63
  replacing screens, 64-65
  spring-loaded, 60, 63
  weatherstripping, 56-59
Wire(s), 36-38
  caulking around, 118
  markings on receptacles or switches, 40
  nut connections, 41
  stripping, 41
Wood,
  blocks for squeaking stairs, 99
  buttons, 10
  caulking, 116-118
  hardwood floor repair, 96-97
  lath, 77
Wooden-frame screens, 65
Wrenches, 6, 15-16, 30-31

X

X-bridging, squeaking floors, 98

Z

Zinc strip, roof maintenance, 107

Cy DeCosse Incorporated offers Black & Decker® Tools at special subscriber discounts. For information write:

  Black & Decker Tools
  5900 Green Oak Drive
  Minnetonka, MN 55343